Death of a Salesman

by Arthur Miller

Curriculum Unit

Jayne R. Smith

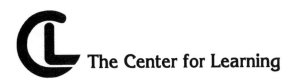
The Center for Learning

Jayne R. Smith, who earned her B.A. and B.F.A. at the University of Oklahoma and M.A. at the University of Texas, has been acclaimed as an English teacher on the secondary level. She is the author of a number of Center for Learning novel/drama curriculum units, including *Cyrano de Bergerac*, *The Old Man and the Sea/Ethan Frome*, *The Martian Chronicles*, *The Joy Luck Club*, and *Bless Me, Ultima.*

The Publishing Team

Rose Schaffer, M.A., President/Chief Executive Officer
Bernadette Vetter, M.A., Vice President
Diane Podnar, M.S., Managing Editor

Cover Design

Clare Parfitt

List of credits found on Acknowledgments
Page beginning on 93.

ISBN 1-56077-234-4

Contents

Introd

The American playwright, Arth
classical definition of tragedy to en
apt hero for tragic drama. In a dem
individual rights, the common per

In *Death of a Salesman*, the author has created a contemporary tragic hero and theme. Willy Loman, derived from Arthur Miller's observations of human behavior of known people, possesses an image of himself which he cannot fulfill within ethical bounds. Tragedy lies in his inability to evaluate himself justly and in the effects of his "dream" image on others. The flow lies in his mistaken view of his rightful status in his world, in his confusion between dreams and reality.

This drama with its motifs of the America dream and ethics is a most important and relevant literary work for today's high school students, living in an era in which national attention is focused on ethical standards at every level of human existence. Students will be drawn into greater awareness of the need for an individual ethical code, without which there is damage to oneself and others.

Beyond the major motifs, this drama offers many other aspects for study: language, music, marital and family relationships, setting, point of view, mini-motifs, omission of humor, and major events of the era.

Teacher Notes

Like most plays, *Death of a Salesman*, should be read aloud. Since setting--and its manipulation—is a key factor to understanding the plot, it is advisable that one student be assigned to read the stage directions. In place of oral reading, an available audio cassette could be used. With either approach, it is wise to stop frequently for questions and/or comments.

The Penguin edition, 1976 reprint, has been used in creating the lesson plans. All page and chapter numbers of other editions used should be checked by the teacher. **Handouts 5** and **8** need to be kept for continuing use.

In this unit, Lessons 1 and 2 introduce students to the topics of Ethics, the American dream, and to the play itself **Handout 9** clarifies time and place and leads into oral reading. The remainder of the handouts are designed to use after the play has been read.

A vocabulary list, which includes many words from the stage directions, is an important aid to reading the play.

Two brief comprehension tests, each covering the entire play, may be useful. For more challenging evaluation, there are selected topics for short essay writing and for lengthier theme writing, preferable to objective testing.

Miller's essay on tragedy, **Handout 34** offers a good study both in content and structure and in recognizing how and why definitions undergo modification. A writing assignment, based on critics' comments, is an option for advanced classes or aspiring writers within a class.

A point of interest to students may be in the author's own comments on his best-known work, written in the years since its publication. They will find contradictions in the origin of the name, Willy Loman. The autobiographical excerpt in *Timebends*, containing the name contradiction, is probably best given to students after the play has been read and discussed.

Dustin Hoffman's TV version of the play is readily available on video. Since the film version is relatively realistic, some elements of the stage version are lost. Therefore, the video, if used, should be shown after this unit is completed.

Lesson 1
Ethics

Objectives
- To focus attention on ethics
- To examine personal ethical positions
- To prepare for analysis of characters' behavior

Notes to the Teacher

The end of the 1980s could be called the *Age of Ethics.* As more and more politicians, judges, stockbrokers, athletes and managers, hotel owners, real estate dealers, and preachers went to trial or jail or both, magazines ran cover stories and special features on ethics, and universities scurried to add ethics courses to curriculums.

Students often read this play in which the code of ethics is frequently broken, with no awareness of the characters' flawed behavior. The first five lessons of this unit will lead students through the often murky maze of ethics and will expect them to think seriously about their own ethics. All of the situations in **Handout 3** involve predicaments of the characters in the play, but they are stated as being those of high school students.

Students may be referred to these situations in later discussion of the play. Almost every lesson will have a reference to Ethics.

Procedure
1. Distribute **Handout 1** for students to read and discuss.

2. Distribute **Handout 2** for individual response and follow-up.

3. Distribute **Handout 3**. Assign one situation to each of five groups. Share responses.

4. Distribute **Handout 4** for homework. State a required length.

5. Distribute **Handout 5** immediately preceding the reading of the play. Tell students to keep it to use in later lessons.
   Suggested Responses:
   Handouts 2 and 3: *Answers will vary.*
   Handout 5: *See chart below.*

Character	Action
Ben	*walked into jungle, came out rich*
Biff	*stole football, pen*
Happy	*takes bribes, seduces boss's fiancé*
Biff and Happy	*steal building supplies*
Willy	*lies to Linda about sales*
Willy	*has a mistress*
Willy	*tells Bernard to give Biff answers on test*
Ben	*trips Biff in fight*
Happy	*leaves work and covers himself*
Howard	*fires Willy*

1

Name _____

Date _____

Good Ole Boys (and Girls) and Ethics

Directions: Read the following items carefully. Answer the questions on **Handout 2**.

A. (from "Harper's Index," *Harper's Magazine*, Sept., 1989, p. 15)
   - Amount Los Angeles transit spent in 1988 on pocketless uniforms to discourage stealing by workers: $10,528.
   - Percentage of fast-food restaurant employees who say they have stolen food or money from their employer: 60 percent.

B. Paul Harvey column, "Customers run up restaurant costs with theft."

C. Ann Landers column, "Thief's luck eventually will run out."

Customers Run Up Restaurant Costs with Theft

In Chicago's western suburb is one of those restaurants good enough to attract visitors from across town and reasonable enough so that neighbors eat there frequently.

It's called *The Homestead*, owned by Ashley Ricketts, whose family has deep roots in Chicago and generations of experience as restaurateurs.

What Ash has tried to do is to provide a dining atmosphere that's borderline elegant; tablecloths and silver silverware, candles, fresh flowers on each table; neat, polite and prompt service and fireplace warmth for those who have to wait.

The meat-and-potatoes menu for the regulars is enhanced by some gourmet specialities--but most significantly, prices are moderate.

Comparable food in comparable surroundings in Chicago frequently runs $40 per person. At the Homestead a similar four-course meal and beverage is closer to $10.

But customers are forcing the prices upward.

I said customers are forcing higher prices--by stealing the silverware.

A restaurant is a microcosm of all industry. Its problems relate to supply, demand, inventory, cash-flow, traffic-handling and race-relations.

And crime.

Mostly the customers are the criminals.

The price of a restaurant meal is increased by the diner who sues because he slipped on a step or because the beans were "too hot."

The price is increased by the diner who empties the basket of rolls into her chairside shopping bag.

Also the butter.

Also the salt and pepper, still in the shakers.

Table decorations where they are not bolted in place.

And ashtrays.

And silverware.

The FBI's crime report says shoplifting increased another 17 percent last year. Other than school-agers, most shoplifters are women between 20 and 50.

The doggie-bag tradition may have encouraged thievery. It is but a short step from taking home uneaten food to taking home appurtenances.

All that government has done to contribute to the something-for-nothing psychology inevitably rubs off on mostly-nice people. Every restaurateur knows some dear souls whom he would not for the world offend, but they are picking the pockets of everybody in the place when they walk off with the cream pitcher.[1]

Thief's Luck Eventually Will Run Out

Dear Ann Landers: My husband has been "bringing" things home from the office for years. I am scared to death that one of these days he will be caught. Lately I've been having nightmares and waking up in a cold sweat.

He has brought home furniture (desks, tables, chairs), tools, office equipment (both manual and electrical) and clothing (uniforms, including pants, shirts, shoes and jackets), which he wears around the house but not to work. How he gets the stuff out is a mystery to me. Either the guards are blind or they are in on it.

I have told him many times I hate to see him bring these things into the house. He looks me straight in the eye and says the business is so big they can afford it and because he has worked for so long "they owe it to me."

At age 40 he is not about to listen to a lecture on morality. His ideas are already formed and I know I can't change him. Our children are too young to understand what is going on, but I worry that one day they will

[1] *Los Angeles Times* Syndicate, March 1982.

discover the truth. When this happens I may have to take them and leave.

I have always been a very scrupulous person, and it is difficult for me to describe the agony I have suffered over this man's lack of integrity.

In most other ways he is a good husband, and believe it or not, he is an excellent father. No one would dream that my husband steals like this from his employer.

Can you offer me some words of wisdom? I feel helpless and trapped and afraid of the future.

--The Wife of a Man With Taking Ways

Dear Wife: You are in a tough spot because you cannot ask anyone to speak to your husband about his "problem" for obvious reasons. Your best hope is to hand him this column and tell him the letter is yours.

I will address myself to this "good husband" and "excellent father," and pray along with you that between the two of us we can reach him.

Dear Friend: This is no lecture. It's just me, dishing out a little common sense.

For years you have been stealing from your employer. Granted, the business is big and the things you lift periodically won't break them. Also granted, you have worked there a long time. But neither of these facts justifies stealing merchandise and equipment. In the eyes of the law, you are a criminal and that's the way you will probably be dealt with.

So far, you've been lucky--but eventually your luck will run out and you will be caught. Every time you steal something you reduce the odds of getting away with it. When you are finally apprehended, your good name will be forever tarnished, you will bring suffering and shame to your wife and children, lose your job (with all the benefits built up over the years), and there is a good chance you will go to jail.

Take a good look at all the things you've stolen over the years. Are they worth your reputation, your family, your job and a stretch in the slammer? I leave it up to you, mister.[2]

---

[2] *Creators* Syndicate, August 30, 1989.

Are You a Criminal?

Directions: These are personal opinion questions. Answer them carefully and honestly. There are no "right" answers.

1. Do you agree with Paul Harvey that taking some little thing from a restaurant is theft and that the taker is a criminal? Why or why not?

2. Are the transit workers and fast-food employees criminals? Why or why not?

3. What about the man who brings home things from his place of employment, as in Ann Landers' column? Is he a criminal? Why or why not?

4. Who pays the actual costs for these types of worker or consumer crimes?

5. Have you or anyone in your family ever taken something from a restaurant, motel (towel, ashtray), schoolroom, or place or work? If so, how did you or he/she feel at the time? What was your/your family member's reason for taking the items?

6. If so, how do you feel now about taking the items? Was this stealing?

7. How would you feel if a friend or neighbor permanently "borrowed" your football, your lawnmower, the material you bought to make something with, your expensive pen?

8. You are now a parent with a school-age son. The child brings home an object which he claims he found somewhere--a baseball mitt, a bicycle, a bracelet. What do you say to him?

9. If you criticized your son for taking something from a restaurant, motel, classroom, or place of employment, and he responded with, "But you bring home stuff from the office all the time. What's the difference," what would your reply be?

10. Do you feel a parent or guardian should set an example in things like consumer theft? Why or why not?

11. Should a parent or guardian reprimand or punish a child who takes little things - a candy bar from a store, an apple from a neighbor's tree, a book from a library? Why or why not?

12. A person's attitude towards right and wrong is his code of ethics. Using your answers to the previous questions as a guide, write in sentence form your ethical position on consumer theft.

Ethics in
Everytown High School, U.S.A.

Directions: Ethics is a system of morals, the choices that must be made between right and wrong. Ethics is more than an attitude towards theft. It enters every aspect of life. Making ethical choices is not easy. The necessity to do so means that everyone is faced daily with ethical problems.

Read the following vignettes. See if you can determine the ethical problem involved. Answer the questions that follow each. There are no "right" answers.

A.
Cathy is a much-admired student leader at school. She willingly gives her time to work on time-consuming activities such as building a homecoming float and making prom decorations. As a cheerleader, she goes to practice everyday and voluntarily helps the students who hope to try out for cheerleader next year. At home she prepares dinner nightly since her mother works. She sometimes baby-sits her sister. She attends church twice a week, sings in the choir, and with her youth group, serves meals to transients every Saturday. On the weekend before her short story for English class is due, Cathy is so busy with activities that she does not have time to write her story. She digs through her mother's collection of magazines, finds an old *Redbook*, and copies a story from it, changing the names of a few places to make it sound as though it takes place in her town. She turns it in, neatly typed, on Monday.

1. Is her action ethical? Why or why not?

2. Do her activities affect your answer at all? If so, why?

3. You are in the same English class. You worked on your story for two weeks rewriting and revising. You earn a *C*; Cathy gets an *A*. You know what she did. How do you feel? What action, if any, do you take?

4. Cathy also cleverly and subtly cheats on tests, but no teacher ever suspects her. As a result, she will be valedictorian instead of you. How do you feel?

5. What do you do?

6. What would you do if her cheating had no effect on your own grade?

      B. Algernon cruises through school, working as little as possible, barely passing, enjoying life, not thinking of the future. Your school has a strict rule that anyone absent for any reason except personal illness or illness in the family must attend detention on Saturday mornings. Algernon likes to sleep late--sometimes until late afternoon. He also likes to go fishing or skiing occasionally on school days. His mother calls the school when he oversleeps or overfishes and says her son is ill. Algernon never has to go to detention.

7. Is the mother's lie acceptable? Why or why not?

8. If you answered "No," would it be acceptable if he were a bright, hard-working student who did four or five hours of homework a night and, after staying up until 3 a.m. working on a physics project, was too exhausted to come to school? Why or why not?

9. If the false excuse were given to your employer so you would not be docked for failing to come to work, would that be acceptable? Why or why not?

      C. Maria is a very attractive girl who uses her looks to her advantage. She discovered at thirteen that she could easily attract any boy she set out to get. By high school years, the game had become too easy so she changed the rules. She set out to capture only males who were already going steady with other girls and who apparently were not interested in anyone else. She had to work a little harder to lure each boy, but she enjoyed the challenge. And she succeeded every time. Once she had succeeded, she dated the boy a few times so that everyone could see her conquest and then dropped him. After she dropped him, she made snide comments about him to her friends and laughed about his inability to resist a pretty female and his lack of loyalty to his original girlfriend.

10. You are the former girlfriend of Butch, the boy she has just taken away and then dropped. How do you feel about Maria?

11. How do you feel about Butch?

12. You are Butch. You have just been dropped by Maria, who you thought was crazy about you. How do you feel about her?

13. Was Maria unethical in any way? Why or why not?

    D. Your best friend, Lisa, went steady all last year with Rob. This year, Rob, who is several years older, broke up with her and later became engaged to Edith. You have discovered that Lisa and Rob are still seeing each other behind Edith's back. You consider this improper behavior.

14. What do you do?
    a. Nothing.
    b. Discuss it with Lisa.
    c. Talk with Rob.
    d. Tell Edith what is going on.

Explain why you made your choice. Whom do you consider more at fault in this situation--Rob or Lisa? Why?

    E. You are basically an upstanding, honest person. While at the mall, you find a wallet on the floor. When you pick it up, you find it contains $100 in cash, plus credit cards, photos, miscellaneous items.

15. What do you do?
    a. Take it to the nearest clerk or store manager.
    b. Take the money and put the wallet back where you found it.
    c. Take the money and turn the wallet in.
    d. Take some of the money and turn the wallet in.
    e. Call the owner.
    f. Take it home and ask your parents what to do.

16. Why did you make your choice?

17. Is it ethical to take money someone else has carelessly lost? Why or why not?

18. Would your answer be different if it were something besides money? Explain.

19. Is it ethical to figuratively take someone's money by not doing your job at work--goofing off, doing something only partway, taking extra breaks, coming late, etc.? Why or why not?

20. Is lying or cheating or stealing or hurting other people acceptable if it helps you to achieve a goal, to become a success? Why or why not?

Name _____

Date _____

Writing about Ethics

Maturity brings increasing awareness that a situation does not have only two alternatives: black or white, good or bad, right or wrong. Often the choices are befogged in gray. Whichever you choose may be partly right and partly wrong.

Ethics presents problems because your standards may differ from those of your friends. People must choose, at times, between doing what they believe is right and doing what will make them popular, accepted or well-liked. It isn't easy to say "no" when your statement may end a friendship, cost you your popularity, or your job.

Ethics become even more difficult when newspapers announce almost daily that highly regarded politicians, businessmen and women, professionals—Gary Hart, Jim Bakker, Pete Rose, and many others—have been caught in unethical acts. Their response is often "But everybody else is doing it!" or "I've done nothing wrong."

Writing about ethics may help you determine your own stand on certain issues. Choose *one* ethical stance or problem (being honest when honesty may get you fired; cheating on an S.A.T. test; being asked by a friend to help her cheat, etc.). Focusing on that issue, write about it. You may write a short story, a personal experience, or an opinion essay. Be as specific as possible.

Alternative Writing Topic: Examine an editorial cartoon which focuses the ideas discussed on the effect of widespread unethical behavior on young people. Write a personal or formal essay on this topic, and include a copy of cartoon, if possible. Be specific in your writing about the unethical behavior satirized and its effects.

Ethics and the Play's Characters

Directions: Fill in this chart as you read the play. Write the character's name and any unethical action or statement *in brief*. Include minor characters such as Uncle Ben and Howard.

Character	Action
Example:	
Biff	stole a carton of basketballs

Save this chart. You will need to refer to it later.

Lesson 2
The American Dream

Objectives
- To recognize the weaknesses in the flawed American dream
- To introduce the dream motif of the play

Notes to the Teacher
This play is a dream play--Willy's dreams of success mingling with his dreams of the past. His dream is the flawed American dream which establishes him as the "common-man hero." The handouts in this lesson acquaint students with American dreams and lead them into the dreams of Willy, the main character.

Procedure
1. Distribute **Handouts 6** and **7** to be done as worksheets. Both **Handouts 6** and **7** can lead to writing assignments on personal goals or the American dream today.

2. Distribute **Handout 8** for students to fill in during play-reading. It can also be used after the play has been read.

Suggested Responses:
Handouts 6 and 7: *Answers will vary.*
Handout 8: *See chart below.*

Optional Activity
A 1989 movie entitled *Field of Dreams*, based on W. P. Kinsella's novel *Shoeless Joe*, is a good enrichment addition to **Handout 8**. Both the movie and novel show the need for dreams, the importance of dreams for survival.

The Iowa part-time farmer, on whose property most of the baseball diamond was built for the film, has left the diamond in the middle of the cornfield. Hundreds of people each week, inspired by the movie's message, travel to the hard-to-find farm to look at or play on the diamond.

Shoeless Joe, a well-written fantasy with J. D. Salinger as a character, is a good novel to teach in conjunction with *The Death of a Salesman.*

Dream	Willy	Biff	Happy
Avoiding manual labor	*scoffs at carpentry*	*enjoys manual labor, ranch work*	*has sales job*
Being a success	*brags and lies about his sales; envies Ben*	*quits jobs when he isn't boss*	*brags and lies about his position*
Helping children be successful	*gives sons advice on getting ahead, getting a loan*	————	————
Investing in material goods	*buys products with big ads, owns own home*	————	*has car, expensive apartment*
Being well-liked	*brags about his popularity; scoffs at Bernard*	*is popular as boy; believes Oliver will remember him*	*considers self charming and irresistible*
Having security	*has life insurance; borrows so he can make payments*	*is at loose ends; has no security*	*seems to enjoy risking his job through seductions, cover-ups, etc.*
Concealing weaknesses	*does not confess adultery; pretends to have sold more than he did; hides suicide attempts*	*does not admit being in jail; forgets he was only stockboy for Oliver*	*pretends to be more important than he is at work*

The American Dream Machine

America! Freedom from persecution; equal justice for all!
America! Home of the free and the brave!
America! Land of opportunity!
America! The streets are paved with gold!
America! Go from rags to riches!
America! Get rich quick!
America! *How to Be a Success in 30 Days or Less*
America! If you're not successful, you're a nobody.

The American Dream, once an honorable goal of freedom, justice, and peace, has, according to many writers and thinkers, disintegrated into a selfish dream of money, success, happiness, eternal youth--a dream that has, in many ways, become a nightmare.

The 1980's have been called "the cynical decade...a time of lowered expectations, heightened self-interest, the triumph of greed over ideals." And the problem is, "so few people can really live out their acquisitive desires, under the circumstances, there is a lot of disillusionment."[1]

Has the American dream collapsed? Rotted away? Turned into cynicism? Was it ever valid? Is the original dream a worthwhile one? Is the selfish dream worthwhile? Is success a desirable goal? What is your American dream?

The Personal Dream Machine

My Goals for the Next Five Years

1. _____
2. _____
3. _____
4. _____
5. _____
6. _____

My Goals for the Distant Future

1. _____
2. _____
3. _____
4. _____
5. _____
6. _____

[1] Donald Kanter and Philip Mirvis, *The Cynical Americans: Living and Working in an Age of Discontent and Disillusion* (San Francisco: Jossey-Bass, 1989).

Name _____

Date _____

Achieving the Dream

Directions: The specific parts of the revised American dream differ from person to person. The following list is not complete, but it contains a number of popular desires. For each one, give proofs or examples (several, if possible) of this desire. Use as examples: yourself, people you know (without naming them), TV, movies, records, advertising, products, industries, etc.

Example:

Having eternal youth	1. Pepsi ads 2. ads for toothpaste, mouthwash, makeup, etc. 3. adults wearing too-young clothing or hairstyles 4. middle-aged men marrying young second wives 5. popularity of spas, exercise videos, etc. 6. Grecian Formula; Retin-A 7. my neighbor's "mod" clothing

A. Avoiding manual labor
   (having a white-collar job)

B. Being a success (often at any price)

C. Helping your children to be more
   successful than you

Name _____

Date _____

D. Investing in material goods (VCR, jewelry, boats, etc.)

E. Being well-liked

F. Having security (life insurance, your own home, good job)

G. Concealing weaknesses

Three Dreamers

Directions: As you read the play, you will discover that there are three dreamers: Willy and his sons Biff and Happy. Many of their dreams are the same as those you have described. Give close attention to Willy's dreams; they are the heart of the play. Fill in this chart as you read the play, and keep it for later discussion. Give specific examples for each person. Some dreams will not pertain to all three characters. In at least one case, a character will *not* believe in one of the dreams.

Dream	Willy	Biff	Happy
A. Avoiding manual labor			
B. Being a success			
C. Helping children be more successful than you			
D. Investing in material goods			
E. Being well-liked			
F. Having security			
G. Concealing weaknesses			

Lesson 3
Willy Loman

Objectives
- To clarify the time/place confusion
- To analyze Willy's character and dreams

Notes to the Teacher

Willy Loman is a controversial character. In equal numbers critics praise and condemn him. He has been called a tragic hero and a pathetic failure, a man to pity, a man who deserves no pity. **Handout 9** places emphasis on how the unusual point of view--inside his head--affects the unrealistic set and the instantaneous shifts in time and place. **Handouts 10-13** put the students inside his head: what is the man like?

Procedure

1. Distribute **Handouts 9 and 10**. Make sure students understand "stage left" and "stage right" so their sketched details will be correct. The sketch in "Suggested Responses" gives an idea of what is expected.

2. Distribute **Handout 11** for students to do individually or in groups.

3. Distribute **Handout 12**. Ask for volunteers to read poems aloud or use poems as choral reading.

4. Distribute **Handout 13**. Use as group discussion. If students have read *The Great Gatsby*, they can discuss further parallels, especially the American dream theme. (There are two theme topics based on a comparison of the two works in "Writing: Theme Topics" in Supplementary Material.)

As students discuss Willy, provide information about Miller's model for Willy. When he was 17 Miller wrote a short story, "In Memoriam," based on his own experiences, in which an old, tired salesman is mistreated by buyers and can sell nothing. The man on whom he based his story committed suicide.
Suggested Responses:
Handout 10:

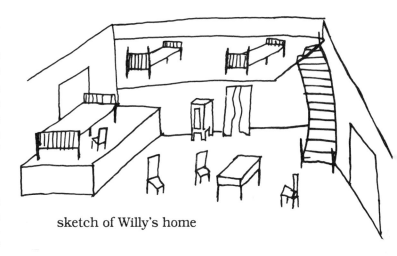

sketch of Willy's home

Handout 11: *See chart on next page..*

Handout 12: *Answers will vary but may include the following:*
A. *Suggests the futility of Willy's living in the past*
B. *Suggests Willy's present situation; the end of the road*
C. *Shows what happens when dreams like Willy's die--the barren field suggests Willy's future. The poem reinforces Charley's statement: "A salesman's got to dream, boy. It comes with the territory."*
D. *Can tie in with the desire for material possessions*
E. *Willy wants to recapture the pleasantness--or seeming pleasantness--of the past; a son who is a popular football hero, a happy home life, sons who adore him, decent sales.*

Handout 13: *Answers will vary.*

Suggested Responses, **Handout 11:**

Willy's Statement	Contradiction
calls Biff lazy	"There's one thing about Biff--he's not lazy."
tells Biff to study math so he won't flunk	"with scholarships...they're gonna flunk him?"
"Chevrolet is the greatest car?"	"That goddam Chevrolet"
"I'm well-liked in Hartford"	"Linda, people don't seem to take to me"
encourages sons to cheat and steal	"I never in my life told him anything but decent things"
condemns Biff's lifestyle	"greatest thing in the world for him was to bum around"
brags about his many friends	tells Charley he is his only friend
"Well, this is the way you're going. Goodbye."	"May you rot in hell if you leave this house!

22

Inside Willy Loman's Head

The Inside of His Head was Miller's original title for the play--and it was an appropriate one. He depicts actual events of the late 1940s and also those of twenty years earlier as they are remembered by Willy.

Willy, in his sixties, tired and under stress, cannot always tell whether he is in the present or the past. Sometimes he addresses someone from the past while he is talking with a present friend or family member. Despite Willy's difficulties in separating the past and present time periods, the author provides several clues so that the reader can tell when he is drifting from the present into the past.

1. Flute music plays as he goes into the past.
2. Trees are projected over the top of his house. (In the present, apartment buildings are shown there).
3. Willy walks through the wall-line (the invisible house wall between the actors and the audience) onto the apron of the stage when in the past. In the present, he walks through the door.

To emphasize unreality, Miller uses an unreal set. Instead of making it look like one room of a house (minus one wall), he shows the entire house with one wall missing. To visualize the set, picture a two-story dollhouse that has been opened by swinging the front of the house to one side. All of the rooms on both floors are visible at one time.

Proscenium Stage

Below you will find a drawing of a proscenium stage, complete with an apron, used for the backyard and several other sites. Draw in details described by Miller.

Keeping the dollhouse in mind, read the stage directions carefully. *Right and left* refer to someone standing on the stage facing the audience. When you complete the sketch, reverse the directions: stage left would be on your right as you face the stage.

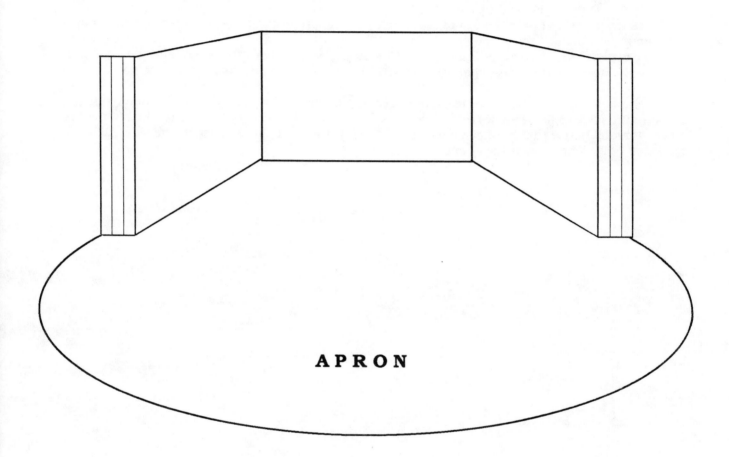

APRON

Death of a Salesman
Lesson 3
Handout 11

Name _____
Date _____

"Very Well, I Contradict Myself"

"I contradict myself? Very well, I contradict myself."
--Ralph Waldo Emerson

Directions: Emerson, a philosopher and poet, believed that a thinking man must contradict himself as he reads and learns more. Only people who do not read, discuss, and think about issues can maintain unaltered opinions. You have undoubtedly read of those who ran for political office supporting a particular issue but later changed positions after learning more about it. However, contradicting oneself is not always commendable. Willy, in his confusion, is frequently guilty of it, whether giving advice, complaining about appliances, or talking to or about people.

List below as many instances as you can find of Willy's contradicting himself. Summarize or quote what he said or did.

Willy's Statement or Action

Example: tells Biff not to pick up anything for Bill Oliver

1. _____

2. _____

3. _____

4. _____

5. _____

6. _____

7. _____

8. _____

Contradiction

Example: picks up Howard's lighter and gives it to him

1. _____

2. _____

3. _____

4. _____

5. _____

6. _____

7. _____

8. _____

What do these contradictions show about Willy?

Name _____

Date _____

Willy and the Dream

Directions: The following 20th-century American poems have lines, themes, etc., that pertain to Willy Loman. Read each one carefully, think about its meaning, and decide how it pertains to Willy. You may need to refer to **Handout 8**, "Three Dreamers."

A. from *John Brown's Body*
     --Stephen Vincent Benet

Only a fool goes looking for the wind
That blew across his heartstrings yesterday,
Or breaks his hands in the obscure attempt
To dig the knotted roots of Time apart,
Hoping to resurrect the golden mask
Of the lost year inviolate from the ground.
Only a fool drives horses in the sky.[1]

B. *The Dump*
     --Donald Hall

The trolley has stopped long since.
There is no motorman.
The passenger thinks
     he is at the end of the line.
No, it is past the end. Around him
     is the graveyard of trolleys,
     thousands of oblongs tilted
     at angles to each other,
     yellow paint chipped.
Stepping outside, he sees smoke rising
     from holes in roofs.
Old men live here, in narrow houses full of rugs,
in this last place.[2]

C. *Dreams*
     --Langston Hughes

Hold fast to dreams
For if dreams die
Life is a broken-winged bird
That cannot fly.

Hold fast to dreams
For when dreams go
Life is a barren field
Frozen with snow.[3]

[1] Stephen Vincent Benet, *John Brown's Body* (New York: Holt, Rinehart & Winston, 1955), 329.
[2] Donald Hall, "The Dump," *The Alligator Bride: Poems New and Selected* (New York: Harper and Row, 1969).
[3] Langston Hughes, *The Dream Keeper* (New York: Alfred A. Knopf).

D. Read this comment by critic Leslie Fiedler:
   "There is only a single industry in the U.S....What that industry produces are not things...but dreams disguised as things: poor vulgar dreams they seem sometimes, but what can one expect of a population descended from the culturally dispossessed of all the nations of the world?"[4]

Discuss how this comment relates to Willy. You might want to consider in your discussion this comment about Willy: Willy buys his own dreams.

E. At the end of his novel *The Great Gatsby*, F. Scott Fitzgerald describes the now-dead Gatsby, a dreamer who had believed he could win back his love and relive the past:

   "Gatsby believed in the green light, the orgiastic future that year by year recedes before us. It eluded us then, but that's no matter--tomorrow we will run faster, stretch out our arms farther...And one fine morning--"

   "So we beat on, boats against the current, borne back ceaselessly into the past."[5]

   How does this description relate to Willy?

[4] Harold Bloom, ed., *Arthur Miller's Death of a Salesman* (New York: Chelsea House, 1988), 50-51.

[5] F. Scott Fitzgerald, *The Great Gatsby* (New York: Scribners, 1961), 182.

Name _____

Date _____

Willy--A Man to Admire?

Directions: Read the following, and answer the questions below.

> Linda tells her sons, "Attention must be paid to such a man...And you tell me he has no character? The man who never worked a day but for your benefit?"
>
> Happy says, "He had a good dream. It's the only dream you can have--to come out number-one man."
>
> Charley says, "Nobody dast blame this man."
>
> At the end of act 2, Willy realizes that Biff not only likes him but loves him.

We have seen how he treats his wife, how he cheats, how he encourages his sons to be dishonest, how he lies about his job and income, how he acts towards his only friend Charley and towards Bernard. Yet, all these people like or love Willy. And, oddly enough, most audiences like him and sympathize with him.

1. Can you explain why?

2. Many people would consider Willy an unethical man. However, Arthur Miller redefines morality in his essay "Tragedy and the Common Man": Moral law is the indestructible will of man to achieve his humanity." "By this definition, what would Miller's view of Willy's morality be?

3. Do you agree with Miller? Why or why not?

Lesson 4
The Salesman: An American Phenomenon

Objectives

- To see the purpose of using a salesman as the American common man
- To perceive the insubstantial nature of white-collar jobs as opposed to blue-collar jobs
- To clarify the association of dreams with salesmen

Notes to the Teacher

Miller not only said that Willy was buying his own dreams, but also that he was selling himself. Charley's speech shows the riskiness of this job, a job dependent on charisma. **Handout 14**, an astounding defense of salesmen, should generate many comments from students. **Handout 15** focuses on the symbolic aspects of "the Salesman." **Handout 17** deals with the ethics of business. The reference to Horatio Alger may need clarification.

Procedure

1. Distribute **Handout 14**. Questions 1 and 2 may be done as class discussion and question 3 as a writing assignment.

2. Distribute **Handout 15** for small group work.

3. Distribute **Handout 16**. Use as class discussion.

4. Distribute **Handout 17**. Use as class discussion.
   Suggested Responses:
   Handout 14: *Answers will vary.*

   Handout 15
   1. *They set Willy up as a symbol.*
   2. *It is unknown.*
   3. *See "Notes to Teacher."*
   4. *He wants a white-collar job.*
   5. *Answers will vary.*
   6. *He seems to be referring to self-esteem, the successful selling of oneself.*
   7. a. *The job is insecure.*
      b. *The job is based on charisma.*
      c. *Answers will vary. Miller wants us to admire the Willy who tried his best but was hampered by society and himself.*
      d. *Answers will vary.*

8. *Answers will vary but may include the drive for success; the futile striving of the American Everyman; the fragility and tenuousness of success.*

Handout 16
1. *His family and Charley come.*
2. *He has no other friends.*
3. *His life is anything but soft and easy; the drive to New England is long, unsuccessful; he is in constant debt. His death was figuratively painless; he was joyous as he drove off, believing he would make Biff rich with the insurance money. (Note that he did not leave the money to his wife.)*
4. *Singleman is <u>not</u> typical, as Willy believes. He is unique. Willy cannot expect to lead his life--or his death. Willy's name, which sounds like "low man," shows his position.*

Handout 17:
1. *He walked into the jungle and came out rich--no effort.*
2. *The event was his unfair attack on Biff. He obviously lied, cheated, perhaps stole and killed to make his fortune.*
3. *They are the ultimate symbol of wealth; a visible symbol.*
4. *It is a business world in which people do not "play fair."*
5. *She is disturbed by him, his fighting, and his attitude towards success. She says, "Why must everyone conquer the world?"*
6. *Charley recognizes the limits a person must stay within. He is not the kind to go outside the law, or to take big risks. Ben sees all successful people as dishonest, a worthwhile characteristic to him.*
7. *Critics disagree. Both can be proved. Miller claimed he did not intend to "put down" businessmen. The makers of the original movie made an introductory "documentary" film in which various salesmen speak and are shown to be exemplary citizens.*

The Salesman in America

Directions: Read the following letter, which appeared in *Changing Times* in 1982 in response to an article about a very young salesman, and respond to the questions below.

Selling the Salesman

I read with great interest your editorial about the 14-year-old salesman ("Chat," May). Being a professional salesman, I envied the experience and presence of mind he had at that young age. I applauded his quick thinking, admired his persuasiveness, envied his closing.

Then came the disappointment. When I read that he wanted to go to a top college and become a scientist, I almost cried. Why, I asked myself, would anyone that talented want to pick a field that is beneath him? If I could talk to that young man, I would try to impress on him that a real salesman can do much more than any scientist, physician or physicist could ever accomplish. A salesman deals with humanity. He is the prime mover for industry, business and people in general. Without the salesman, everything would come to a stop. Sadly, in today's society, few, if any, remember this important fact of life.

--Don Rothy
Winter Park, Fla.

1. Judging only from the evidence in this letter, characterize the writer.

2. Would Willy agree with his attitude towards salesmen? Explain.

3. Write a letter agreeing or disagreeing with the writer's view of a salesman. Be more specific than the writer; give examples, proofs. Begin with "Dear Editor."

Name _____

Date _____

Willy, the Salesman

Directions: Respond to the questions below.

1. Notice that Arthur Miller calls his play *Death of a Salesman*, not *Death of Willy Loman*. Before Willy first enters, the stage directions say, "Before us is the Salesman's house." (Note the capital *S*). Then they say, "From the right, Willy Loman, the Salesman, enters carrying two large sample cases."

    What is the significance of these directions? Why the capital *S*?

2. What product does Willy sell?

3. Why doesn't Miller name the product?

4. Willy, who is excellent at carpentry, chooses instead to be a salesman, a job at which he has apparently never been very good. Thinking of the discussion about the American dream, why did he make this job choice?

5. In act 2, Willy tells Ben, "It's contacts, Ben, contacts!...that's the wonder of this country, that a man can end with diamonds here on the basis of being liked." To his sons he says, "Because the man who makes an appearance in the business world, the man who creates personal interest, is the man who gets ahead. Be liked and you will never want."

    To what extent is a salesman's success related to his appearance and his ability to make friends? Why are these surface elements, with no relationship to the product or its quality, important to a salesman?

6. In the same scene, when Ben invites Willy to go to Alaska, he asks, "What are you building? Lay your hand on it. Where is it?" Willy, after admitting there is nothing, then gives his "contacts" speech, ending with, "You can't feel it with your hand like timber, but it's there!" The comparison is between construction and sales work. What does Willy's response mean?

7. At the end of his life Willy is a failure. According to Linda, "He drives 700 miles, and when he gets there no one knows him anymore, no one welcomes him."

   Willy, who had "the wrong dreams," according to Biff, kills himself to fulfill another dream--making Biff rich through insurance money, which he can "pick up and touch in [his] hand. Not like--like an appointment." Since the insurance company knows about his earlier purposeful accidents, even this dream is unfulfilled. Yet, Charley, a successful businessman, delivers a moving requiem for Willy.

   Nobody dast blame this man. You don't understand: Willy was a salesman. And for a salesman, there is no rock bottom to the life. He don't put a bolt to a nut, he don't tell you the law or give you medicine. He's a man way out there in the blue, riding on a smile and a shoeshine. And when they start not smiling back--that's an earthquake. And then you get yourself a couple of spots on your hat, and you're finished. Nobody dast blame this man. A salesman is got to dream, boy. It comes with the territory.

   a. Why is there "no rock bottom to the life" of a salesman?

   b. What does the metaphor "riding on a smile and a shoeshine" mean?

   c. Why would Charley, who knows all of Willy's shortcomings, say, "Nobody dast blame this man?"

   d. Look at Charley's last two sentences. "The territory" refers to the area a salesman covers. Why do you think a salesman has to dream? Relate your answer to your responses for questions 5, 6.

8. Think about the assertion in question 1 that Willy is "the Salesman"--the embodiment, perhaps of all salesmen, all Americans (the salesman is an American invention) who hold similarly amorphous jobs dependent less on talent, education, and training than on easily changed factors, such as a spot on a hat. If Willy is a kind of metaphor for an American trait or an element of the American dream, what is that trait or element? Explain.

Name _____

Date _____

Dave Singleman: The Death of a Salesman

Directions: Read the following quotes, and answer the questions.

In act 2, Willy tells Howard about Dave Singleman, the eighty-four-year-old salesman, who inspired Willy and who "died the death of a salesman, in his green velvet slippers in the smoker of the New York, New Haven and Hartford, going into Boston--when he died, hundreds of salesmen and buyers were at his funeral."

When Willy, at the end of act 2, speaks to the imaginary Ben about his impending suicide, he says, "Ben, that funeral will be massive! They'll come from Maine, Massachusetts, Vermont, New Hampshire! All the old-timers with the strange license plates--that boy will be thunderstruck, Ben, because he never realized--I am known!...He'll see what I am, Ben! He's in for a shock, that boy!"

1. Who comes to Willy's funeral?

2. What earlier comment has Willy made to Charley that helps explain this?

3. A critic, D.L. Hoeveler, has defined the myth of the American dream as "an easy, soft life and an easy, painless death!" Has Willy achieved either of these? Explain.

4. Why would Miller have chosen the name *Singleman* for the ideal salesman? What about Willy's name suggests he was not destined for Singleman's glorified death and funeral?

Two Successful Businessmen

Directions: Willy has two models of business success to follow if he wishes, men he knows, as opposed to Dave Singleman. His neighbor, Charley, who lends Willy money that will never be repaid, frequently offers Willy a job, and feels no urge to be popular, although he is quite successful. Willy does not see him as admirable.

His brother, Ben, whom he almost worships, is a scoundrel with money and rarely visits him. Unlike Howard, who inherited his father's business, both Charley and Ben are self-made men.

1. In what sense is Ben the epitome of the classic Horatio Alger rags-to-riches story?

2. What event gives us the idea of how he achieved his wealth? How did he achieve it?

3. Why did Miller use diamonds as the source of Ben's wealth?

4. Metaphorically, in terms of business, what could be meant by Ben's walking into a jungle?

5. What is Linda's reaction to Ben? What does she think of his job offer?

6. Interpret what the interchange below reveals about each of the two successful businessmen:
   Charley: Willy, the jails are full of fearless characters.
   Ben: And the stock exchange, friend!

7. Which of the two men do you believe Miller considered more typical of the American businessman? Give proof.

Lesson 5
Money, Ethics, and Business

Objectives
- To allow application of understanding ethics
- To recognize the problems in making ethical decisions
- To direct attention to the ethical values of the characters

Notes to the Teacher
This lesson applies the ideas of Lesson 1 to the play. In **Handout 18**, students will discover that it is not easy to label a character as ethical or unethical. **Handouts 19 and 20** alert them to the complicated ethics of the business world. Some critics believe one of Miller's main statements in the play is criticism of American consumerism. Explain *subliminal advertising*.

Procedure
1. Distribute **Handout 18**. It may be done individually or in groups of 3 or 4.

2. Distribute **Handout 19** for small group work.

3. Distribute **Handout 20**. Number 1 calls for an individual response. Others may be used for group or class discussion.
   Suggested Responses:
   Handout 18: *Answers will vary.*
   Handout 19
   1. sales--using his mistress to get to the buyer
   2. perhaps through stealing; expects to be #1 man in any job; steals his way out of every job
   3. his job--taking bribes, demeaning his superiors, etc.
   4. the jungle--methods suggested by the umbrella point above Biff's eye
   5. his unfairness and dishonesty
   6. Just before he says this (p. 25) he tells how he takes bribes from salesmen who want an order.

Handout 20
1. List will vary.
2-7: Answers will vary.
8. his mistress; his lies to Linda about his job and his earnings
9. Answers will vary. The firing is certainly unfair (but is it unethical?) with no mention of benefits, retirement, etc., after long years of service. A business cannot support an employee who does not do his work or is unsuccessful in it. Howard calls Willy, many years his elder, "kid," demeaning him. He shows a lack of sympathy but is not unethical.
10. Answers will vary.
11. See #9.
12. his failure to make sales
13. A business has a responsibility to its employees.
14. very likely the reason Charley gives-- jealousy; embarrassment at the idea of having to work for the man he always considered beneath him
15-16. Answers will vary.
17. The market for products would be almost nonexistent if everything lasted "forever." However, changing styles, "improvements," additives, etc., aided by advertising hype, tempt people to buy new cars and appliances when their old ones still work.

Name _____

Date _____

Back to Ethics I

Directions: Reread your ethics list in **Handout 4.** Now, make some ethical judgments. For each character, write a few sentences proving him/her to be ethical or unethical. If characters demonstrate both qualities, prove so. Use proofs from your list or from the play.

1. Willy

2. Biff

3. Happy

4. Charley

5. Howard

6. Linda

7. Ben

After completing your mini-paragraphs, exchange papers with another student or another group. If you disagree in any of your judgments, discuss what you said and defend your point of view. Do not let your personal feelings for the character enter into your argument.

8. Discuss: Was Willy's suicide an ethical act? How would he defend it? What is unethical about it?

Back to Ethics II: Get Rich Quick

Directions: One of the American slogans you encountered earlier was "Get rich quick!" Think how many people in America believed in that possibility--the shortcut to wealth: Horatio Alger's rags-to-riches tales; the people in the Gold Rush; farmers who moved to the rich city; pioneers who moved West; bootleggers; aspiring movie and television actors and athletes; conniving manufacturers; slick Wall Street brokers; former White House aides; purchasers of lottery tickets; gamblers.

How does each of these characters hope to get rich quick? What dishonest or unethical means does he use? (use phrases)

1 Willy

2. Biff

3. Happy

4. Uncle Ben (the play's symbol for this quality)

5. After Ben's unfair fight with Biff, Ben says, "Never fight fair with a stranger, boy. You'll never get out of the jungle that way." What do the fight and the comment reveal about Ben and his ethics?

6. Happy says to Biff, "You know how honest I am." Explain the irony.

Name _____

Date _____

Business Ethics

Directions: Read the following, and answer the questions.

Unethical acts in the workplace are, unfortunately, not uncommon. Think of examples of unethical practices in your hometown or those you have read about or seen on TV. Subliminal advertising, now ostensibly illegal, is one example. Have you ever been lured into a store by a "Big Sale," only to find that the item isn't quite what it was advertised to be? Have you been sold shoddy merchandise? Has a repairman done a poor job at a high cost?

1. List your examples here.

    a.

    b.

    c.

    d.

    e.

    f.

    g.

2. Why might businessmen have done some of the unethical things you have listed?

A business must make money or close. Is it ethical for a business to do these things:

3. raise prices?

4. release employees?

5. charge customers for employee or customer theft?

6. sell shoddy merchandise?

7. lure customers in with prizes or questionable sales?

8. What evidence do we have that Willy was unethical in his job?

9. Was it ethical for Howard to fire Willy, a long-time employee who was no longer making sales? Why or why not?

10. Should a business put profits above people? Vice-versa? Explain.

11. What would Howard's logical reason be for releasing Willy?

12. In what sense did Willy deserve to lose his job?

13. In what sense is he right when he tells Howard, "You can't eat the orange and throw the peel away --a man is not a piece of fruit"?

14. Why wouldn't Willy accept a job from Charley?

15. Was it ethical for him to tell his wife that the money borrowed from Charley was his salary? Why or why not?

16. Is it ethical for businesses to manufacture appliances, such as Willy's refrigerator, or cars that are intended to work for only a certain length of time? (The practice is called "planned obsolescence.") Why or why not?

17. If refrigerators, light bulbs, toasters or cars lasted for a long time, what effect would that have on manufacturers? Is planned obsolescence necessary in order to keep manufacturers and retail stores in business?

Lesson 6
Biff, The Golden Boy

Objectives
- To discover the validity of the American desire to be successful
- To examine Biff's character
- To see the effects of unethical behavior

Notes to the Teacher
In this lesson, Biff's character is examined primarily in terms of ethics. Since he is the only character in the play who changes, he is sometimes considered the main character. Students may wish to discuss the symbolism of Biff's burning his University of Virginia tennis shoes.

Procedure
1. Distribute **Handout 21** for small group work.

2. Distribute **Handout 22** as a homework assignment. The writing can be evaluated or read to the class for comparisons of views of Biff's character.

3. Distribute **Handout 23**. Use as class discussion.
   Suggested Responses:
   Handout 21
   1 and 2: Answers will vary. As part of number 2 use the poem "Richard Cory" by Edwin Arlington Robinson.
   3. *It is his desperate attempts to relive his past with no audience except the candy wafers.*
   4. *Biff, in all his jobs, tries to be #1 just as he was in high school, but fails at all of them.*

   Handout 22
   1. *Suggested choices.*
      a. *"Coach'll probably congratulate you on your initiative."*
      b. *"Because the man who makes an appearance...is the man who gets ahead. Be liked and you will never want."*
      c. *To Bernard: "You'll give him the answers."*
      d. *"You want him to be a worm like Bernard?"*
      e. *He sends the boys off to steal sand and lumber.*

   f. *He disappointed Biff with the Woman.*
   2. *He was possibly getting even for the disillusionment scene.*
   3. *Essay answers will vary.*

   Handout 23
   1. *He can accomplish anything.*
   2. *She is a buyer whose room is being painted.*
   3. *She puts him through to the buyer. This is probably not ethical.*
   4. *His mother has to mend her stockings. Willy promised her new ones.*
   5. *He had idolized his father and has discovered the clay feet.*
   6. *Hap probably would not have reacted that strongly if at all. Happy takes after his father in personality.*
   7. *He acts on the pretense of being a good person, of setting a good example for his boys.*
   8. *He gave up, burned his shoes, did not go to summer school.*
   9. *They could no longer communicate or bear to be around each other for very long.*
   10. *Answers will vary. Most may consider Willy more ethical. They need to recognize why Biff's desire is a form of dishonesty.*
   11. *Yes--Biff shows his love by returning home, agreeing to see Bill Oliver, lying about his visit when he learns of his father's firing, dashing out of the restaurant and speaking to Hap before he leaves.*
   12. *Yes--Willy shows his love by his nervousness when Biff returns, his pushing him to apply for a loan, his reaction when he realizes Biff loves him, his reason for his suicide.*
   13. *His dream was to be #1. He failed because of his attitude and because he was, according to his own analysis, always second-rate. Answers to the last part of the question will vary.*

Name _____

Date _____

We're #1!

Directions: Read and respond to the following items:

Is there a single athletic team in America that is not considered number 1 by its fans? Bumper stickers proclaim, "We're number 1!" Supporters at games wave enormous foam hands with raised index fingers to say the same thing. No one wants to be last--or even number 2.

Is losing a sin? Is failure a disgrace? Is *winning* the name of the game? Many people believe that, in America, the answer to all of these questions is "Yes!" When the game changes from football to life, the answer remains the same.

Sometimes the desire to be number 1 causes otherwise good people to do unethical things. Athletes take steroids; bright students cheat on tests; politicians use smear tactics; hotel owners cheat on taxes.

1. List other specific examples of unethical actions to be number 1 in school, business, music, politics, banking, sports, etc.

a. _____

b. _____

c. _____

d. _____

e. _____

f. _____

g. _____

2. Aside from unethical acts, what other problems can result from the desire to be number 1?

Have you ever considered what happens when a person is no longer number 1, when he has peaked too soon, too young? Read this poem about an athlete who starred in high school but went nowhere.

Ex-Basketball Player
John Updike

Pearl Avenue runs past the high school lot,
Bends with the trolly tracks, and stops, cut off
Before it has a chance to go two blocks,
At Colonel McComsky Plaza. Berth's Garage
Is on the corner facing west, and there,
Most days, you'll find Flick Webb, who helps Berth out.

Flick stands tall among the idiot pumps-
Five on a side, the old bubble-head style,
Their rubber elbows hanging loose and low,
One's nostrils are two S's, and his eyes
An E and O. And one is squat, without
A head at all--more of a football type.

Once, Flick played for the high-school team, the Wizards.
He was good--in fact, the best. In '46,
He bucketed three hundred ninety points,
A country record still. The ball loved Flick.
I saw him rack up thirty-eight of forty
In one home game. His hands were like wild birds.

He never learned a trade; he just sells gas,
Checks oil, and changes flats. Once in a while
As a gag, he dribbles an inner tube.
But most of us remember anyway.
His hands are fine and nervous on the lug wrench.
It makes no difference to the lug wrench, though.

Off work, he hangs around Mae's Luncheonette.
Grease-grey and kind of coiled, he plays pinball,
Sips lemon cokes, and smokes those thin cigars;
Flick seldom speaks to Mae, just sits and nods
Beyond her face towards bright applauding tiers
Of Necco Wafers, Nibs, and Juju Beads.[1]

3. What makes Flick pathetic?

4. In what ways is he like Biff?

[1] John Updike, *The Carpentered Hen and Other Tame Creatures* (New York: Harper and Row, 1957).

Name _____

Date _____

I'm Number 1!

Directions: Read and respond to the following:

> [Biff] comes downstage into a golden pool of light.
>
> WILLY: Like a young god. Hercules--something like that. And the sun, the sun all around him...God Almighty, he'll be great yet. A star like that, magnificent, can never really fade away!
>
> This *was* Biff, the high-school football hero--"a crowd of girls behind him everytime the classes change," his friends willing to sweep out the furnace room for him, college scouts fighting over him: a winner.
>
> BIFF: Pop! I'm a dime a dozen, and so are you...I'm not a leader of men, Willy, and neither are you...I'm one dollar an hour, Willy! I tried seven states and couldn't raise it. A buck an hour! Do you gather my meaning? I'm not bringing home any prizes any more, and you're going to stop waiting for me to bring them home.
>
> This *is* Biff, the thirty-four year-old unemployed ex-prisoner who steals his way out of every job he gets; the employee who can't endure not being the boss: a loser.

1. Biff accuses his father of causing his failure, of filling him full of hot air. List below some specific things Willy did or said to the young Biff that could have led to his later actions and his failure in life:

   a. _____

   b. _____

   c. _____

   d. _____

   e. _____

   f. _____

2. Several times Willy accuses Biff of "spiting" him. Was he right?

3. Biff is a dynamic character, the only character in the play who changes in some way. Write a brief characterization of Biff, showing him before and after the change. What event causes this change? Discuss only the adult Biff.

Disillusionment

Directions: Be prepared to answer the following questions:

The climactic scene of the play occurs at the restaurant when Willy finally remembers the disastrous visit of Biff to Willy's Boston hotel room.

1. Biff came to Boston in order to get his father to talk to his math teacher about changing his grade. What does this show about Biff's opinion of his father?

2. What is Willy's excuse for having the Woman in his room?

3. What does the Woman do for Willy at the office where she works? Is this ethical?

4. Why is Biff so horrified at the gift Willy gives the Woman? Give several references from earlier in the play.

5. Why is Biff so completely crushed by his discovery? Be specific.

6. Would Happy have reacted the same way? Why or why not?

7. Why does Biff call Willy a fake?

8. How did this scene affect Biff's immediate future (after high school)?

9. How did it affect his future relationship with his father?

10. Consider the ethical problems in this scene: Biff's reason for coming--wanting Willy to do something unethical--Willy's affair. Who is the worse offender? Are there degrees of being unethical? Explain your choice.

11. Does the adult Biff love his father? Give several proofs, not just Willy's statement near the end. Explain why, if he did love him, he walked out of the restaraunt.

12. Does Willy love the adult Biff? Give several proofs.

13. Examine Biff's comments in act 2 and the Requiem about his and his father's dress. Discuss him as a dreamer; of what did he originally dream? Why did his dreams fail? Is he right about Willy's dreams? Is Happy wrong?

Lesson 7
Family Relationships

Objectives
- To examine father-son relationships
- To examine the validity of the importance of popularity

Notes to the Teacher
In today's world of broken families, this topic may lead in unexpected directions or arouse intense feelings. Keep the discussion of the Ann Landers' column concentrated on the two applicable sections: the paragraphs about not pleasing the father and the unrealistic demands of the father.

In **Handout 25** Happy's name can be discussed. Students may have difficulty in understanding Happy's declarations in the Requiem after his treatment of Willy in the restaurant. Happy is neither consistent nor logical, but a romantic like his father. The discussion of child-rearing methods may evoke controversy.

Procedure
1. Distribute **Handout 24** for small group work. After completing the handout, ask students to assume the persona of Biff, Happy, Willy, or Linda. Write a letter to Ann Landers about a problem he/she faces in the play. Write Ann's reply.

2. Distribute **Handout 25** for individual work.

3. Distribute **Handout 26** for individual or small group work.
   Suggested Responses:
   Handout 25
   1. to do as little as possible and yet get ahead; ducking out during work hours; taking bribes; lack of respect
   2. seducing their fiancés
   3. considers them all prostitutes, though he is always the aggressor
   4. as a boy he admires him--his reaction when his father comes home, his pleas for attention; as a man, it varies--helps a little financially, plans to follow Willy's dream, walks out on Willy, denies he is his father

5. "He's not my father. He's just some guy." He is perhaps concerned for Biff, or more likely, his thoughts are with the girls and Willy is becoming an embarrassment.
6. Answers will vary but may include his romantic view of life, his inability to understand Willy's flaws.
7. It is very unlikely. He will lie or cheat and be unwilling to work steadily.
8. This is the younger-child syndrome. He isn't as impressive as his older brother. It would make him admire his father more or resent him without realizing it.
9. Answers will vary.
10. Answers will vary.

Handout 26
Charley
a. said his son did things, never bragged
b. warned Willy about these actions, so obviously did not allow son to do so
c. "never took an interest in anything"
d. same as c
e. admired his son, treated his as an equal
1 and 2. Answers will vary. Critics disagree. His not encouraging unethical activities and his not lying about his son apparently resulted in a successful son.
3. He is embarrassed and unwilling to admit Biff's failure (failure is a sin to him).
4. Biff is incapable of accomplishing anything but, like Willy, talks big. Bernard acts. Willy equates talking with action. Charley, a modern Spartan, believes one does what he should.

Name _____
Date _____

Sons and Fathers

Husband's Expectations Unrealistic

Dear Ann Landers:

My husband and I have raised a large family, each child very different from the other. They range from extremely ambitious to somewhat unmotivated.

Our children received different levels of education. Some have been more successful careerwise than others, but on the whole, they have chosen pleasant spouses, brought up respectful, caring youngsters and have managed to get along quite well financially with occasional help from us.

I truly believe, especially in this day and age, that we have been blessed. We have never had any earthshaking problems with any of our children or grandchildren, or with each other.

My husband (I'll call him "Dan") feels we have failed as parents because "Mary" doesn't keep an immaculate house, or "John's" car is never clean, or "Joan" spends money on frivolous things, or "Bill's" kids have atrocious manners and talk with gum in their mouths.

I keep reminding him that it's quite extraordinary to have had 40 years of marriage and no major calamities in a family of our size. A few hurt feeling here and there, but no big blowups.

As the years fly by, I see Dan becoming more obsessed with "unmet expectations." He nurses his angry feeling and becomes increasingly bitter. He doesn't realize that he is not perfect and that he has not always fulfilled *my* "expectations."

Dan quit going to church because the minister wasn't "spiritual" enough. He openly encourages the children (especially the adult males) not to attend church. I love to walk, jog and dance. Dan will not join me in these activities because he "gets enough exercise at work." So I jog, walk and go to church alone.

My future looks bleak. It is possible that I will be a widow with financial burdens because Dan has a good chance of dying from lung cancer before he is 60. The man lights one cigarette off the other and refuses to quit.

If the cigarettes don't get him, I see myself growing old with an increasingly angry and bitter man, complaining more and more because everyone has failed him.

Ann, please do a column on expectations, real and unrealistic. I keep telling Dan that you can't change people, but he says I'm wrong.

I believe this is the reason so many adults (mostly males) say, "No matter how hard I tried, I could never please my father." The result is disappointed parents and unhappy children.

I hope my letter will touch a tender spot in some of your readers. Please encourage children and spouses to clip and mail this column to the offending member of the family.

--Ever Prayerful, Ever Hopeful in Middle America

Dear Middle America:

I suspect your husband's dissatisfaction with his children is rooted in the fact that he never received unconditional love and approval from his own father.

The unrealistic demands he makes on his sons and daughters are the result of his unfulfilled dreams. He wanted his children to be perfect because he never was. Of course, they failed him, and he feels "cheated."

Unless Dan gets some therapy (highly unlikely), your prognostications may well be correct. I hope that you are as strong as you seem to be and that you will continue to maintain a positive attitude and continue to count your blessings, no matter what.[1]

Although this letter describes a different situation than the one Biff faced, find some points in both the letter and the reply that apply to the relationship between Biff and Willy.

In groups of three or four, discuss this letter, the answer, and any parallels you find.

---

[1] *Creators* Syndicate, 18 January, 1989.

Name _____
Date _____

"Hey, Pop! Please Notice Me!"

Directions: Answer the following questions:

Although he has a pleasant, eager personality, it is hard to admire Happy. Prove this by stating his attitude towards the following and giving examples:

1. His job

2. His bosses

3. Women

4. His father

Your answer to number 4 may include some contradictory elements since Happy is inconsistent in his attitude toward Willy. Perhaps his most shocking comment was made to the two girls just before they left the restaurant.

5. How do you explain this statement and his action of leaving? Consider the fact that Willy has told them he has lost his job and "the woods are burning."

6. How do you explain Biff's anger in the Requiem when he says that Willy had the wrong dreams and his statement that Willy "had a good dream. It's the only dream you can have--to come out number 1 man. He fought it out here, and this is where I'm gonna win it for him."

7. From the evidence in the play, will Happy become number 1 man? Explain.

8. Happy is obviously not number 1 with his father, who dotes on Biff. Several times in the play, both as a youth and an adult, he repeats, "I lost weight, Pop, you notice?" and "I'm getting married." Neither parent ever responds to his statements. What does this show about Happy? What effect might it have on his character?

9. Look at **Handout 5**. What unethical actions or statements do you have listed for Happy that have not been mentioned? Is he a totally unethical person? Why or why not?

10. Is his father to blame for his character? Why or why not?

Name _____

Date _____

What's the Secret?

Who is admired more--the athlete hero or the brightest student? What lies ahead for most intellectuals? For most high-school athletes?

The athlete in the play is Biff, and the scholar is Bernard. Do their names suggest their personalities? Willy calls Bernard a pest and "an anemic." Biff assures his father that Bernard is "liked, but he's not well-liked." Willy becomes irritated when Bernard tells Biff to study. Before the big game, Bernard begs to carry Biff's shoulder guards so that he can get into the locker room.

Fifteen years later, the ex-football hero is a loser, so frustrated by his realization that he is not the type of person one gives loans to that he steals his former boss's fountain pen and runs down eleven flights of stairs.

Look at the "ex-wimp!" He is not only a lawyer, but has also achieved the ultimate goal of lawyers: arguing in front of the Supreme Court. Instead of cowboys, he has friends who live in elegant homes with private tennis courts. He is married and has a family. Willy, who had laughed at the "wimp," asks Bernard's father, "What's the secret?"

What is the secret? From clues in the play, what can you determine about the way Charley reared his son? Contrast Charley's child-raising methods with Willy's.

Willy	**Charley**
a. bragged on his son's accomplishments	a. _____
b. encouraged his sons to cheat and steal	b. _____
c. was a buddy to his sons	c. _____
d. supported his sons' activities	d. _____
e. worshipped Biff	e. _____

1. Are Charley's methods of child-rearing ideal ones? Why or why not?

2. In what ways are his methods--or some of them--preferable to Willy's?

3. Why does Willy lie to Bernard about what Biff is doing now?

4. Bernard does not tell Willy about the Supreme Court appearance; his father does. Willy says, "The Supreme Court! And he didn't even mention it!" Charley replies, "He don't have to--he's gonna do it." Discuss how this brief interchange points out the difference between Biff and Bernard as well as the difference between Willy and Charley.

Lesson 8
It's a Man's World

Objectives
- To analyze Linda's character
- To observe how traits can be variously interpreted
- To investigate the sin of inaction

Notes to the Teacher
A feminist reading this play might be highly offended by both the attitude and treatment toward women and the women's acceptance of their status. Linda, much admired by many readers, especially in her powerful speeches supporting Willy, can also be viewed as a passive person, who allows her sons to be reared unethically.

Procedure
1. Distribute **Handout 27** for class discussion.

2. Distribute **Handout 28**. Assign as a written response or as an informal debate.

3. Distribute **Handout 29** to be done as homework and shared in class discussion.
   Suggested Responses:
   1. *Her life is one that has many problems. Instead of seeking a new life (divorce?) she mends her problems by pacifying Willy, keeping the sons from disturbing him, allowing him to err and even to kill himself. (Students might find other things the stockings might symbolize.)*
   2. *He remembers the woman and his gift of new stockings.*
   3. *Her attitudes are forgiving and accepting—receiving his revised sales numbers calmly; putting the rubber hose back; speaking to the boys about him, etc.*
   4. *They are far secondary to Willy. She invites them to leave if they plan to disturb Willy. She is a realist (Biff resembles her eventually) who sees them for what they are. She calls Happy a "philandering bum."*
   5. *She lacks Willy's drive for success.*
   6. *She merely accepts each new figure and says, "That's very good."*
   7. *She can't insult him by stopping him. Answers will vary on the ethical question.*
   8. *No, she is a realist. She rejects Ben.*
   9. *Their life was a constant attempt to get paid up. Now that they are, he is dead and, it seems, life in the paid-for house will be meaningless.*
   10. *He often tells her to shut up; yells at her.*

Handout 29

Name	Occupation	Revealing Actions	Male Who Uses Her
The Woman	*buyer*	*"I picked you"; "We do have such a good time together"; "I love a lot of stockings"; You are the saddest, self-centeredest soul I ever did see-saw."*	*Willy*
Miss Forsythe	*model*	*"I have been [on a cover]" "I could make a phone call"*	*Happy*
Letta	*?*	*"Isn't he cute? Sit down with us, Pop." "I think it's sweet to bring your daddy along."*	*Happy Biff?*
Charlotte	*?*	*goes out with Hap after she is engaged*	*Happy*

61

2. They are all easily available.
3. No, he is the aggressor. He takes pride in capturing them and then degrades them, and all womanhood.
4. She tells Biff that she is a football, figuratively--something to be kicked around.
5. They are people to be enjoyed, to use, to discard. (Biff is less so than the others, although their discussion of Big Betsy makes him part of the family attitude.)

Name _____

Date _____

Linda: The Loyal Wife

The item, perhaps a symbol, most commonly associated with Willy's loyal wife Linda is stockings. In the pre-nylon age, silk stockings were expensive, an appreciated gift. Women repaired runners with special thread.

- Linda is always mending her stockings.
- The other woman gets gifts of stockings from Willy.

1. If the constantly mended stockings are taken as a metaphor for Linda's life with Willy, what do they reveal? What actions of hers are "mending" ones?

2. Why does Willy get furious when he sees her mending stockings?

3. What is Linda's attitude towards Willy? Give several examples, including the introductory stage directions.

4. What is her attitude towards her sons? Give several examples.

5. What does her reaction to Ben reveal about her?

6. How does she react, in a memory scene, when Willy lies to her about how much he earned? Explain her reaction.

7. Why does she keep replacing the rubber hoses that she knows are intended for suicide? Is she right to do this?

8. Is she a dreamer? Why or why not?

9. She is constantly making payments or paying for repairs. What is the irony in her final speech, directed to Willy: "I made the last payment on the house today...Any there'll be nobody home. We're free and clear"?

10. In act 1, she tells her sons that she loves Willy. Aside from his affair, which she knows nothing about, what does he say to her that makes it questionable that he really loves or appreciates her? Does his comment to his sons, "The woman has waited and the woman has suffered," affect your answer?

Name _____
Date _____

Linda, The "Stupid Wife"

Read this comment by Brian Parker.

> Her appeal to traditional values and her downtrodden loyalty are, however, apt to blind audiences to the essential stupidity of Linda's behavior. Surely it is both stupid and immoral to encourage the man you love in self-deceit and lies...Linda does not really believe his dreams--at least not at the point where we meet her, whatever she may have done earlier; but, without any higher ideals than Willy, she humors him to keep things going...After 35 years of marriage, Linda is apparently completely unable to comprehend her husband; her speech at the graveside...is not only pathetic, it is also an explanation of the loneliness of Willy Loman which threw him into other women's arms.[1]

Respond to this interpretation of her character. Support or refute Parker's statement using specific proofs from the play.

[1] Brian Parker, "Point of View," *The University of Toronto Quarterly* 35., No. 2, January, 1966.

Name _____

Date _____

The Other Woman
--and Women in the Play

Whatever position you take on Linda's character, you must admit that the other women in the play--those who appear and those talked about--do not qualify as admirable.

1. Fill in the chart below with brief quotations or descriptions of actions for the four women listed.

Name	Occupation	Revealing Comments or Actions	Male Who "Uses" Her
The Woman			
Miss Forsythe			
Letta			
Charlotte (act 1)			

2. What do these ladies have in common?

3. When Miss Forsythe goes off to call a friend, Happy says to Biff, "Isn't that a shame now? A beautiful girl like that? That's why I can't get married. There's not a good woman in a thousand." Is Happy right in putting the blame on the various women he seduces? Why or why not?

4. The Woman seems a willing partner in her affair with Willy. How does Miller make her sympathetic?

5. How would you describe the attitude of the three Loman men towards women?

Lesson 9
Men of the World

Objectives
- To observe how men in superior positions affect Willy
- To clarify Willy's state of mind in the planting scene
- To clarify Howard's insensitivity

Notes to the Teacher
This lesson concentrates on two important scenes in act 2, both of which lead to Willy's tragic end. Investigating the effects of these two powerful men on Willy when he is most defenseless helps to understand the final tragedy.

Procedure
1. Distribute **Handout 30**. Ask students to reread pp. 76-84 before answering questions.

2. Distribute **Handout 31**. Reread pp. 125-127; pp. 133-135. Answer questions.
   Suggested Responses:
   Handout 30
   1. To Willy, it suggests a closeness, an importance to Howard's father--part of the past. To Howard, it is trivial since it has nothing to do with his skills or sales.
   2. He has a lack of sensitivity, an air of superiority. Students may see a parallel to white people's, in an earlier era, addressing adult black males as "Boy."
   3. It reveals his insensitivity again, disinterest, a habit of bragging to any audience. Willy, who can't even afford a car radio for his frequent long trips, is used to lying about his finances and pretending to be affluent.

4. Both men boss their wives and worship their children. Miller may be showing that Willy's qualities are common to all levels of society-- the more affluent may steal or cheat in more subtle, sophisticated ways, but are actually just like Willy.
5. Howard treats his act of firing a long-term employee as if it were a minor nuisance, cured by a brief rest.
6. He can no longer keep up the pretense of bringing home a salary; he cannot pay his bills; he is totally defeated.

Handout 31
1. a. The speeches are no longer about going to Alaska or Africa.
   b. Ben listens carefully to Willy and responds to his ideas instead of preaching.
   c. Ben doesn't brag.
   d. Ben looks at his watch as usual, but discovers he has a little time.
   e. His "jungle" line is changed.
   f. Ben encourages Willy.
   g. Ben says, "We'll be late" instead of "I'll be late."

2. It is not a memory scene as the others were. Willy has "created" Ben to discuss his problem with.
3. Willy is actually arguing with himself while remembering the dead Ben's earlier promise of diamonds (the insurance money).
4. He is out of his last dream and realizes he has to make the final decision.

Name _____
Date _____

Howard

Directions: Answer the questions below.

Howard, like Ben and Charley, is a successful businessman, although he apparently inherited his position and his wealth from his father, Willy's original boss.

1. Whether true or not, Willy keeps reminding Howard that he named him. Why is that fact important to Willy and unimportant to Howard?

2. Several times Howard calls Willy "kid." What does that reveal about Howard?

3. After Howard tells Willy that he is going to throw out all his technical "toys" and just play with his new wire recorder, Howard says, "Sure, they're only a hundred and a half. You can't do without it...You tell the maid to turn the radio..." Howard employs Willy and knows his tenuous financial situation. What does this speech reveal about Howard? What does Willy's pretense that he might buy one reveal about him?

4. Howard plays his wire recorder for Willy, who also has a fascination for mechanical things: cars, refrigerators. What does the recording show that Howard and Willy have in common concerning their wives and their children?

5. What is ironic about Howard's advice to Willy after he fires him: "Sit down, take five minutes, and pull yourself together..."?

6. How does this scene lead to Willy's suicide?

The Other Ben

Directions: Reread pp. 125-127 and 133-135 before answering the questions.

In the 1920's Ben makes two visits to Willy's house, visits which Willy recreates in the present. During these times he offers Willy a job in Alaska, repeats his success formula ("When I was 17 I walked into the jungle and when I was 21 I walked out. And by God I was rich"), and offers questionable advice. He is obviously Willy's ideal, his model. He is also dishonest, as discovered in a previous lesson.

The memory of these visits gives Willy inspiration when his life turns sour. But Ben, always in a hurry, disappears when Willy wants to continue talking. He walks off into the darkness.

At the end of act 2, Ben reappears while Willy plants seeds that have no chance to grow. This scene occurs after his sons desert him in the restaurant, after he remembers the event that turned Biff against him, after he has been fired. Although Ben leaves when Biff enters, he returns after Willy learns that Biff loves him.

1. Reread these last two scenes with Ben. List at least five things that are different from the earlier appearances of Ben:

   a. _____

   b. _____

   c. _____

   d. _____

   e. _____

   f. _____

2. What assumption can you make about this appearance of Ben's, based on these differences?

3. In effect, with whom is Willy discussing his imminent suicide?

4. After his "elegy" to Biff ("Now when you kick off, boy…") he realizes he is alone and asks, "Ben! Ben, where do I…? Ben, how do I…?" What do these questions show?

Lesson 10
Tragedy

Objectives
- To review the elements of a tragedy
- To introduce the possibility of a 'common-man' hero
- To link the motifs of ethics, dreams, and tragedy

Notes to the Teacher

Not everyone agrees with Miller's premise that the play is a tragedy. However, students need to understand Miller's reasoning for this premise. Miller's essay, in the *New York Times*, shortly after the first reviews in 1949, is difficult for students to understand, since he never connects his arguments directly to the play. Reading the essay is not required in order to do **Handouts 32** or **33**. It is included in **Handout 34** to use with advanced classes or as a challenge with any student level of ability. It may also be read aloud and discussed paragraph by paragraph. Some teachers may prefer to use it for their own information.

Procedure

1. Since this lesson is a cumulative one, designed to make students integrate ideas from the entire play, **Handouts 32** or **33** should be done in small groups.

In **Handout 33**, question 10 should be answered individually. It may be developed into a paragraph or used as a debate topic. Suggested Responses:

Handout 32
1. *Social position: high (prince, king)*
   Qualities: nobility, courage, loyalty to countrymen, perseverance
   Weaknesses: often an excess of a good quality (too trusting, too ambitious); hubris (overwhelming greed)
   Goal: to correct a wrong, to achieve a good
   Fate: defeat in his goal or death
2. *Social position: lower middle class*
   Qualities: devotion to sons; dishonesty,

disloyalty to wife; ambition
   Weakness: dishonesty; his dream for his sons
   Goal: to make his sons successful
   Fate: unsuccessful sons; suicide
3. *Answers will vary.*

Handout 33
1. *Answers will vary.*
2. *Answers will vary.*
3. *He would perhaps respond that nobility has a different meaning to an ordinary man: Willy believed he was giving his life for his son.*
4. *His death is sad; the audience is led to this opinion by the sound effects, the music, and the Requiem. But Willy dies happy.*
5. *Answers will vary.*
6. *People witnessed his suicide attempts and the insurance company knows about them. Biff will not get the money since the death was a suicide. Willy is defeated even in death.*
7. *The entire play is his progress toward death, his reasons for it (compare to Sir Thomas Malory's L'Morte de Arthur).*
8. *Answers will vary. Willy, like most people, was tempted and misled by ads, aspired to be what he was incapable of becoming ("Everyone can become President"), set shallow goals. These may have doomed him to defeat.*
9. *Answers will vary. Give students this portion of a definition of tragedy from Benet's Readers' Encyclopedia (Harper & Row, 1987):*
   "In modern tragedy, the emphasis is not so much on a struggle against fate or some tragic flaw but on a conflict with social, hereditary, psychological, or environmental forces."
10. *Answers will vary.*

Tragedy in America

Directions: Define and compare tragic heroes.

You have probably read at least one classical tragedy: *Romeo and Juliet* or *Macbeth, Oedipus the King* or *Medea.* If so, you know the "rules" for a tragedy. What do you expect of the tragic hero?

1. Social position:

   Qualities:

   Weaknesses:

   Goal:

   Fate:

2. Think about Willy Loman and chart the same terms:

   Social position:

   Qualities:

   Weakness:

   Goal:

   Fate:

3. Compare Willy to one classical tragic hero, such as Oedipus, Brutus, Macbeth, or Romeo. Show both similarities and differences.

The Common Man
as Tragic Hero

Directions: Read Miller's viewpoint, and answer questions that follow.

> Since America has no kings or princes, it seems unlikely that a classical tragedy could be written here. But Arthur Miller, in his 1949 essay entitled "Tragedy and the Common Man," defends the possibility of an ordinary American having the qualities of a tragic hero. Miller believes that a common man "is as apt a subject for tragedy in the highest sense as kings were"; that a common man can think, aspire, suffer; and that a common man can give his life for "his sense of human dignity."

1. Do you agree with Miller? Why or why not?

2. A tragedy must arouse the audience's pity and fear in order for *catharsis* (a purging of emotions) to occur. Does Miller's play accomplish this? Explain.

3. Many critics accuse the play of merely arousing pathos--they feel sorry for Willy but do not feel he died nobly or that he suffered for a high cause. How might Miller respond to this argument?

4. There is usually a sadness at the end of a tragedy when the hero, despite his efforts, dies or realizes his failure. In what way is this true about Willy? In what way is it not true?

5. Can a play which ends happily for the hero be a tragedy? Why or why not?

6. Willy is joyous as he goes to his death. What does he fail to realize? Does that make his joy tragic?

7. Why has Miller entitled his play *Death of a Salesman?* (Why not call it *Life of a Salesman?*) Why is it "a Salesman," not "the Salesman"?

8. In Greek tragedies there is often Fate controlling the lives and destinies of the tragic figures. One feels that no matter what the hero does, he is doomed to fail. In what sense could society--its values, its requirements, its expectation, and its temptation--serve as Willy's Fate?

9. In what sense are Willy's dream and his unethical behavior causes of his tragedy?

10. Do you consider the play a *tragedy* and Willy a *tragic hero?* Explain.

Tragedy and the Common Man

Arthur Miller

In this age few tragedies are written. It has often been held that the lack is due to a paucity of heroes among us, or else that modern man has had the blood drawn out of his organs of belief by the skepticism of science, and the heroic attack on life cannot feed on an attitude of reserve and circumspection. For one reason or another, we are often held to be below tragedy--or tragedy above us. The inevitable conclusion is, of course, that the tragic mode is archaic, fit only for the very highly placed, the kings or the kingly, and where this admission is not made in so many words it is most often implied.

I believe that the common man is as apt a subject for tragedy in its highest sense as kings were. On the face of it this ought to be obvious in the light of modern psychiatry, which bases its analysis upon classified formulations, such as the Oedipus and Orestes complexes, for instances, which were enacted by royal beings, but which apply to everyone in similar emotional situations.

More simply, when the question of tragedy in art is not at issue, we never hesitate to attribute to the well-placed and the exalted the very same mental processes as the lowly. And finally, if the exaltation of tragic action were truly a property of the high-bred character alone, it is inconceivable that the mass of mankind should cherish tragedy above all other forms, let alone be capable of understanding it.

As a general rule, to which there may be exceptions unknown to me, I think the tragic feeling is evoked in us when we are in the presence of a character who is ready to lay down his life, if need be, to secure one thing--his sense of personal dignity. From Orestes to Hamlet, Medea to Macbeth, the underlying struggle is that of the individual attempting to gain his "rightful" position in his society.

Sometimes he is one who has been displaced from it, sometimes one who seeks to attain it for the first time, but the fateful wound from which the inevitable events spiral is the wound of indignity, and its dominant force is indignation. Tragedy, then, is the consequence of a man's total compulsion to evaluate himself justly.

In the sense of having been initiated by the hero himself, the tale always reveals what has been called his "tragic flaw," a failing that is not peculiar to grand or elevated characters. Nor is it necessarily a weakness. The flaw, or crack in the character, is really nothing--and need be nothing but his inherent unwillingness to remain passive in the face of what he conceives to be a challenge to his dignity, his image of his rightful status. Only the passive, only those who accept their lot without active retaliation, are "flawless." Most of us are in that category.

But there are among us today, as there always have been, those who act against the scheme of things that degrades them, and in the process of action everything we have accepted out of fear or insensitivity or ignorance is shaken before us and examined, and from this total on-slaught by an individual against the seemingly stable cosmos sur-rounding us--from this total examination of the "unchangeable" envi-ronment--comes the terror and the fear that is classically associated with tragedy.

More important, from this total questioning of what has previously been unquestioned, we learn. And such a process is not beyond the common man. In revolutions around the world, these past thirty years, he has demonstrated again and again this inner dynamic of all tragedy.

Insistence upon the rank of the tragic hero, or the so-called nobility of his character, is really but a clinging to the outward forms of tragedy. If rank or nobility of character was indispensable, then it would follow that the problems of those with rank were the particular problems of tragedy. But surely the right of one monarch to capture the domain from another no longer raises our passions, nor are our concepts of justice what they were to the mind of an Elizabethan king.

The quality in such plays that does shake us, however, derives from the underlying fear of being displaced, the disaster inherent in being torn away from our chosen image of what and who we are in this world. Among us today this fear is as strong, and perhaps stronger, than it ever was. In fact, it is the common man who knows this fear best.

Now, if it is true that tragedy is the consequence of a man's total compulsion to evaluate himself justly, his destruction in the attempt posits a wrong or an evil in this environment. And this is precisely the morality of tragedy and its lesson. The discovery of the moral law, which is what the enlightenment of tragedy consists of, is not the discovery of some abstract or metaphysical quantity.

The tragic right is a condition of life, a condition in which the human personality is able to flower and realize itself. The wrong is the condition which suppresses man, perverts the flowing out of his love and creative instinct. Tragedy enlightens--and it must, in that it points the heroic finger at the enemy of man's freedom. The trust for freedom is the quality in tragedy which exalts. The revolutionary questioning of the stable environment is what terrifies. In no way is the common man debarred from such thoughts or such actions.

Seen in this light, our lack of tragedy may be partially accounted for by the turn which modern literature has taken toward the purely psy-chiatric view of life, or the purely sociological. If all our miseries, our indignities, are born and bred within our minds, than all action, let alone the heroic action, is obviously impossible.

And if society alone is responsible for the cramping of our lives, than the protagonist must needs be so pure and faultless as to force us to deny his validity as a character. From neither of these views can tragedy

79

derive, simply because neither represents a balanced concept of life. Above all else, tragedy requires the finest appreciation by the writer of cause and effect.

No tragedy can therefore come about when its author fears to question absolutely everything, when he regards any institution, habit or custom as being either everlasting, immutable or inevitable. In the tragic view the need of man to wholly realize himself is the only fixed star, and whatever it is that hedges his nature and lowers it is ripe for attack and examination. Which is not to say that tragedy must preach revolution.

There is a misconception of tragedy with which I have been struck in review after review, and in many conversations with writers and readers alike. It is the idea that tragedy is of necessity allied to pessimism. Even the dictionary says nothing more about the word than that it means a story with a sad or unhappy ending. This impression is so firmly fixed that I almost hesitate to claim that in truth tragedy implies more optimism in its author than does comedy, and that its final result ought to be the reinforcement of the onlooker's brightest opinions of the human animal.

For, if it is true to say that in essence the tragic hero is intent upon claiming his whole due as a personality, and if this struggle must be total and without reservation, then it automatically demonstrates the indestructible will of man to achieve his humanity.

The possibility of victory must be there in tragedy. Where pathos rules, where pathos is finally derived, a character has fought a battle he could not possibly have won. The pathetic is achieved when the protagonist is, by virtue of his witlessness, his insensitivity, or the very air he gives off, incapable of grappling with a much superior force.

Pathos truly is the mode for the pessimist. But tragedy requires a nicer balance between what is possible and what is impossible. And it is curious, although edifying, that the plays we revere, century after century, are the tragedies. In them, and in them alone, lies the belief--optimistic, if you will, in the perfectibility of man.

It is time, I think, that we who are without kings, took up this bright thread of our history and followed it to the only place it can possibly lead in our time--the heart and spirit of the average man.[1]

[1] Arthur Miller, "Tragedy and the Common Man," (New York: Viking Press, 1949).

Writing: Answering the Critics

This play has had three Broadway productions: the original one with Lee J. Cobb in 1949; the 1975 production with George C. Scott; and the 1984 production with Dustin Hoffman (later taped for television). In 1983 it was even successfully presented, in Chinese, in China. Although American critics were unable to evaluate the Chinese version, many expressed their views about the other productions.

Read these excerpts carefully. Choose *one* to respond. Write the excerpt as the first paragraph of your paper, using quote marks. Agree or disagree with the critic. Use specific examples to prove your point.

1. "Miller had the makings of some sort of play; but he was unfortunately unable to bring a single spark of dramatic intelligence to bear on his material....(The play) proceeds, with unrelieved vulgarity, from cliche to stereotype. The language is entirely undistinguished...; the tone of the play can best be described as a sustained snivel."[1]

2. "Its theme comes across with blinding clarity--failure is the only sin Americans will not forgive."[2]

3. "Thematically, too, the play is cloudy. It's hard to believe that, centrally, Miller had anything more than muzzy anti-business, anti-technology impulses in his head....The figure (of Willy) that comes through the play is not of a man brought down by various failures but of a mentally unstable man in whom the fissures have increased."[3]

4. "The double attitude of the play toward Willy--depicting him as selfish and foolish while insisting that he's noble and good--reads like a man's failed attempt to portray sympathetically the father he wants to forgive but can't."[4]

[1] Frederick Morgan, "Notes on the Theatre," (New York: The Hudson Review, 1949), 272-273.

[2] T. E. Kallen, *Time*, 7 July 1975.

[3] Stanley Kauffman, *New Republic*, 19 July 1975.

[4] Lloyd Rose, "Lost in America," *Atlantic*, April 1984.

Writing: Theme Topics

1. Choose one of the following and develop topics into a well-organized theme.

   a. Willy's dream affected the lives of both sons.
   b. In his plays, Miller attacks American ethics and standards.
   c. Miller uses Charley and Bernard as contrasts to Willy and Biff.
   d. Willy's immorality leads to his defeat.
   e. Willy's death is/is not a tragic one.
   f. Linda is/is not an admirable person.
   g. Uncle Ben represents the flawed American dream.
   h. Willy's quest for the American dream leads to his defeat.
   i. Uncle Ben, Charley, and Howard embody contrasting values as businessmen.

2. Characterize Biff, Willy, or Linda. For prewriting, make a list of the character's qualities. Then list several specific events or actions that illustrate each quality.

3. Compare Willy's or Ben's unethical approach to success with that of some well-known figure of today who has obtained success in similar ways (government officials, bankers, TV evangelists, Wall-Street brokers, etc.).

4. The play is full of irony. Find several examples and discuss the purpose and effect.

5. Do you believe a common man can be tragic? If so, write a personal essay (use first person) giving your reasons and describing at least one ordinary person you know or know of whose character and life make him both noble and tragic by Miller's definition.

6. You are Biff. After your father's funeral, you realize you need to return Bill Oliver's pen. A letter of explanation must, of course, accompany the pen. Write the letter, consistent with Biff's character and his newly-found realization about himself.

7. You are Howard. After Willy's dismissal, you write a report explaining the reason for firing him after 35 years. Be consistent with Howard's character.

8. Charley tells Willy that Bernard doesn't have to talk about being successful because he _is_ successful. Create an imaginary high-school student who is like Biff--all talk, no achievement. Place him in a situation in which he is forced to recognize what he is. Write as a scene from a story.

9. Several things in the play could be considered symbols; the gas hot-water heater, the flute music, the stockings, the Salesman, the refrigerator. Choose two or three and discuss them as symbols.

10. The point of view, from inside Willy's head, is most unusual, coloring the way characters are shown, merging past into the present. Discuss Miller's point of view and its effectiveness.

12. Willy believed a person must be well-liked. Is that true today? Discuss the importance (or unimportance) to a high-school student of being well-liked.

13. Another American dreamer is Jay Gatsby in F. Scott Fitzgerald's *The Great Gatsby*. Compare Willy to Gatsby in terms of their dreams: what they were, how they sought to achieve them, and the results of their achievements.

14. Compare Willy to Gatsby in terms of ethics. How and why did each man break ethical codes? To what degree was each aware of what he was doing? Considering their ethical lapses, how does each character evoke sympathy?

15. Read Robert Frost's narrative poem "Death of a Hired Man." Compare similar elements in the poem and the play (aside from the similar titles). Consider the hired man, his unreliability and his attitudes, the feelings of the couple towards him, the ideas about home, the use of nature, etc.

16. Miller uses music frequently in his play, from the flute music and the father who used to make flutes, to the music used at the end of act 2 to suggest the crash. Find all the references to music in the play and write a paper in which you suggest what Miller intended to accomplish through the inclusion of music.

17. A person's use of language often reveals a great deal about him. Howard, as he listens inattentively to Willy and then fires him, speaks in cliches. Examine his cliches and their context and explain what this language reveals about Howard.

18. Willy is a man of contradictions, from his statements to his actions. Discuss what these contradictions show about Willy's character.

Death of a Salesman: Comprehension Test I

Answer each question in a word or phrase.

1. What phrase did Happy keep repeating? (2 possibilities)

2. How did Uncle Ben become rich?

3. What special position did Bernard achieve in later life?

4. Who was Dave Singleman?

5. What did Linda find--and leave where it was?

6. What did Biff steal at the office where he went for money?

7. For what *real* reason did Biff not go to college?

8. What was Willy doing in the backyard at the end when he saw Ben?

9. Which character finally realized the truth about the people in the family?

10. What can Linda not do at the funeral?

Name _____

Date _____

Death of a Salesman: **Comprehension Test II**

1. What did Willy have the boys do when he got home from his trip (when they were boys)?

2. What did he bring the boys?

3. What did Uncle Ben ask Biff to do?

4. Why did Biff go to Bill Oliver's Office?

5. What career did Bernard choose?

6. What argument, besides years of work, did Willy use with Howard for keeping his job?

7. What did Willy object to about Charley's rearing of Bernard?

8. Why did Happy leave Willy in the restaurant?

9. At the end of the play, why was Willy happy before he went back into the garden?

10. In the graveyard, what good news did Linda have for Willy?

Answer Key to Comprehension Tests

Part I	Part II

Part I

1. "I'm losing weight" or "I'm getting married."
2. by going into the jungle
3. arguing before the Supreme Court
4. the old salesman who died the death of a salesman
5. a rubber pipe on the gas water heater
6. a fountain pen
7. his discovery about his father
8. planting seeds
9. Biff
10. cry

Part II

1. wash the car or hang up clothes
2. punching bag
3. go to Alaska--work for him
4. to get a loan
5. law
6. he named him
7. no interest in his son
8. to follow Biff or to be with the girls
9. Biff loved him.
10. They were free and clear. The house was paid for.

Name _____

Date _____

Vocabulary List: *Death of a Salesman*
(Penguin Edition)

Act I

mercurial 12

trepidation 12

resigned 13

accommodating 14

crestfallen 15

reminiscences 16

infinite 17

agitation 22

insinuates 27

immersed 28

incipient 30

initiative 30

tauntingly 32

subsiding 38

incarnate 41

laconic 41

valise 44

stolid 44

aura 44

dispel 46

audacity 52

simultaneously 59

feasible 63

subdued 65

Act II

incredulously 88

frenzy 90

ominously 122

implacably 122

contemptuous 132

idyllic 133

elegiacally 135

An Excerpt from Miller's
Autobiography *Timebends*

Willy Loman based on a real uncle of Miller's

Arthur Miller's most famous play, *Death of a Salesman*, is rooted in his childhood experiences. In this third part of a five-part series, Miller describes how he found the model for Willie Loman within his own family.

By Arthur Miller

I actually spent no more than a couple of hours in my Uncle Manny's presence in my life, but he was so absurd, so completely isolated from the ordinary laws of gravity, so elaborate in his fantastic inventions, and despite his ugliness so lyrically in love with fame and fortune and their inevitable descent on his family, that he possessed my imagination until I knew more or less precisely how he would react to any sign or word or idea. His unpredictable manipulations of fact freed my mind to lope and skip among fantasies of my own, but always underneath was the river of his sadness.

In those days, before the parkways and superhighways, a traveling salesman had to drive through every town, stop at every traffic light, and he carried a short-handled shovel in the trunk to dig his way out of drifts, since there were no snow tires as yet and many towns only plowed their roads once in a storm.

It was the unpredictability of his life that wove romance around it. He was not in some dull, salaried job where you could never hope to make a killing. Hope was his food and drink, and the need to project hopeful culminations for a selling trip helped, I suppose, to make life unreal.

Much more than a single model would ultimately go into Willy Loman. Indeed, since I saw so little of Manny he was already, in my youth, as much myth as fact.

Manny had managed to make his boys into a pair of strong, self-assured young men, musketeers bound to one another's honor and proud of their family. Neither was patient enough or perhaps capable enough to sit alone and study, and they both missed going to college. Buddy joined the Seabees during the war and welded landing mats for aircraft on Pacific islands, married an older woman who had her own children, and died at 40 of cancer, an entrepreneur at last, serving aircraft workers sandwiches from a small fleet of vans he had managed to buy or lease. Abby fought with the infantry at Anzio.

The last I saw of Abby was a number of years before he died, in his early 40s, like his mother, of hypertension. He had invited me to his bachelor apartment in Manhattan after I phoned him. I had not seen him since before the war. Wearing blue silk pajamas and slippers, he ushered me into his small living room overlooking lower Lexington Avenue.

"What did your pop want?" I asked him. This was what I had come for.

I was obsessed these days by vague but exciting images of what can only be called a trajectory, an arched flow of storytelling with neither transitional dialogue nor a single fixed locale, a mode that would open a man's head for a play to take place inside it, evolving through concurrent rather than consecutive actions. By this time I had known three suicides, two of them salesmen. I knew only that Manny had died with none of the ordinary reasons given.

"I mean if you had to say the one thing he wanted most, the one thing that occurred to him most often, what would it be?"

"He wanted a business for us. So we could all work together," my cousin said. "A business for the boys."

This conventional, mundane wish was a shot of electricity that switched all the random iron filings in my mind in one direction. A hopelessly distracted Manny was transformed into a man with purpose: He had been trying to make a gift that would crown all those striving years; all those lies he told, all his imaginings and crazy exaggerations, even the almost military discipline he had laid on his boys, were in this instant given form and point. To be sure, a business expressed his own egotism, but love, too.

It was an accidental meeting almost a year earlier that had set me up for the particular question I asked and for the resonances of the answer my cousin gave. On a late winter afternoon I had walked into the lobby of the old Colonial Theater in Boston, where *All My Sons* had just opened, its Broadway premiere a few weeks away, and I was surprised to see Manny among the last of the matinee audience to leave.

"Manny! How are you? It's great seeing you here!"

Without so much as acknowledging my greeting, he said, "Buddy is doing very well." Then I saw a passing look of embarrassment on his face, as though, perhaps, he had not always wished me well.

We chatted for a moment, and he went out of the vast lobby and into the street. I thought I knew what he was thinking: That he had lost the contest in his mind between his sons and me. An enormous welling sorrow formed in my belly as I watched him merge into the crowd outside. Collected in his ludicrous presence was all of life.

But it was the absence of the slightest transition to "Buddy is doing very well" that stuck in my mind; it was a signal to me of the new form that until now I had only tentatively imagined could exist. I had not the slightest idea of writing about a salesman then, totally absorbed as I was in my present production. But how wonderful, I thought, to do a play without any transitions at all, dialogue that would simply leap from bone to bone of a skeleton that would not for an instant cease being added to, an organism as strictly economic as a leaf, as trim as an ant.

And more important than even that, a play that would do to an audience what Manny had done to me in our surprising meeting--cut through time like a knife through a layer cake or a road through a mountain revealing its geologic layers, and instead of one incident in one time frame succeeding another, display past and present concurrently, with neither one ever coming to a stop.

One afternoon, after attending to some business in midtown, I was about to head for the subway and a bit of warmth when my eye caught *The Testament of Dr. Mabuse* on one of the 42nd Street marquees. I decided to look in on it again. It was one of the films that over the years since I had first seen it had become part of my own dream tissue and had the same intimacy as something I had invented myself.

The dingy theater at 3 o'clock in the afternoon was almost empty. Even worse, I had been making preliminary sketches of scenes and ideas for a salesman play and should have been home at my desk. I was still at the stage of trying to convince myself that I could find a structural arch for the story of the Lomans, as I called the family. The name had appeared suddenly under my hand one evening as I was making my vagrant notes. "Loman" had the sound of reality, of someone who had actually lived, even if I had never known anyone by that name.

Now, watching Fritz Lang's old film, I was drawn into the astounding tale, gradually recalling it from the past. From time to time, Paris is experiencing fires, derailments, explosions, but the chief of the *Surete* is baffled because he can find no motive for these catastrophes, which he has come to believe are not accidental but the work of criminals. But to what end and for whose profit he cannot imagine. He visits a great psychiatrist, Dr. Mabuse, who heads a famous clinic outside Paris. The doctor explains that indeed these are probably not accidents but that the perpetrators will be very difficult to find. They may be people of all classes who have one thing in common--a disgust with civilization and the wish simply to destroy it. Being psychological and moral, the profit is impossible to track.

The chief, played by Otto Wernicke, proceeds to send out men to keep watch on the crowds that collect at fires and other calamities. In time, one young detective notices a man watching a particularly awful fire in an orphanage and recalls having observed him at a previous fire. He begins to track this fellow and is led into a great printing plant closed for the night. The detective finds himself in a basement auditorium that is about a quarter filled with men and women representing every class of people in Paris, from pretentious business types to common laborers, students and shopkeepers. They seem unrelated and sit quite apart from one another, all watching a curtain drawn across a stage. From behind it now is heard a voice that in quiet, rather businesslike tones instructs the audience on the next objective, a Paris hospital that is to be dynamited and set afire. The detective rushes the stage, parts the curtain--and discovers a phonograph playing a record. The chase is on.

He slips into a tiny office, quietly shuts the door, switches on the light and sits down at a phone to call the chief. The camera moves into a close-up on the young detective's desperate face as he clamps the receiver to his ear and whispers, "Hello? Hello! Lohmann? Lohmann!" The light snaps out and the screen goes black before he can give his location. The next shot finds him in an asylum in a white gown, seated on a bed with his hand up to his ear gripping a non-existent phone receiver, a look of terror in his face, repeating, "Lohmann? Lohmann? Lohmann?"

My spine iced as I realized where I had gotten the name that had lodged so deep in me. It was more than five years since I had last seen the film, and if I had been asked, I never could have dredged up the name of the chief of the *Surete* in it. In later years I found it discouraging to observe the confidence with which some commentators on *Death of a Salesman* smirked at the heavy-handed symbolism of "Low-man." What the name really meant to me was a terror-stricken man calling into the void for help that will never come.

Source: Arthur Miller, *Timebends* (Grove Press Inc., 1987).

Bibliography

Bloom, Harold, ed. *Arthur Miller's Death of a Salesman.* Modern Critical Interpretations Series. New York: Chelsea House, 1988.

Corrigan, Robert W., ed. *Arthur Miller. Twentieth Century Views.* Englewood Cliffs, N.J.: Prentice Hall, Inc., 1969.

Downer, Alan S., ed. *American Drama and Its Critics.* Chicago: University of Chicago, 1965.

Martine, James J., ed. *Critical Essays on Arthur Miller.* Boston: G.K. Hall and Co., 1979.

Miller, Arthur. *Arthur Miller's Collected Plays, with an Introduction.* New York: Viking Press, 1957.

——————— *Death of a Salesman.* New York: Viking Press, 1949.

——————— *Salesman in Beijing.* New York: Viking Press, 1984.

——————— *Timebends: A Life.* New York: Grove Press, 1987.

Moss, Leonard. *Arthur Miller.* Boston: Twayne Publishers, 1980.

Weales, Gerald. *American Drama Since World War II.* New York: Harcourt, Brace and World, 1962.

Video

Miller, Arthur. Death of a Salesman. Irvine, Calif.: Karl-Lorimar Home Video, Inc., 1986.

Miller, Arthur. Death of a Salesman. 135 min. color.
Starring Dustin Hoffman and John Malkovich.
Zenger Media, 10200 Jefferson Blvd., P.O. Box 802, Culver City, CA 90232-0802

Filmstrip

Death of a Salesman, Color filmstrip, review and analysis, discussion guide and student evaluation. Filmstrip/cassette. DR43CFX. Listening Library, Inc. Old Greenwich, Conn.

Audio-Cassette

Death of a Salesman, Lee J. Cobb and Mildred Dunnock. 2 cassettes. DR41cX. Listening Library, Inc. Old Greenwich, Conn.

Acknowledgments

For permission to reprint all works in this volume by each of the following authors, grateful acknowledgment is made to the holders of copyright, publishers, or representatives named below.

Lesson 1, Handout 1
"Customers Run Up Restaurant Costs..." by Paul Harvey. © 1989, Los Angeles Times Syndicate. Reprinted by permission.

Lessons 1, 7, Handouts 1, 24
"Thief's Luck Will Eventually Run Out" by Ann Landers. Copyright by Creator's Syndicate. August 30, 1989. "Husband's Expectations Unrealistic" by Ann Landers. Copyright by Creator's Syndicate, January 18, 1989.

Lesson 3, Handout 12
Excerpt from *John Brown's Body* by Stephen Vincent Benet, 1955. published by Holt, Rinehart & Winston, New York, New York.

"The Dump" by Donald Hall. Copyright © 1969 by The New Yorker Magazine Inc., from *The Alligator Bride: Poems New & Selected* by Donald Hall. Published by Harper & Row Publishers, Inc., New York, New York.

Lesson 3, Handout 12
"Dreams" from *The Dream Keeper and Other Poems* by Langston Hughes. Copyright 1932 by Alfred A. Knopf, Inc. and renewed 1960 by Langston Hughes. Reprinted by permision of Alfred A. Knopf, Inc.

Whole Book
Excerpts from *Death Of A Salesman* by Arthur Miller, 1966. Copyright 1966 Arthur Miller. published by Viking-Penguin Inc., New York, New York.

Lesson 4, Handout 14
Excerpt from "Selling the Salesman" by Don Rothy from *Changing Times Magazine*, July, 1982. Reprinted with permission from *Changing Times Magazine*, July, 1982. © Kiplinger Washington Editors, Inc., July, 1982.

Lesson 6, Handout 21
"Ex-Basketball Player" from *The Carpentered Hen And Other Tame Creatures* by John Updike. Copyright © 1957, 1982 by John Updike. Reprinted by permission of Alfred A. Knopf, Inc.

Lesson 8, Handout 28
Excerpt from "Point of View in Arthur Miller's *Death of a Salesman*" by Brian Parker from *University of Toronto Quarterly 35*, No. 2 (January, 1966). Reprinted by permission of University of Toronto Press, Toronto, Canada.

Lesson 10, Handout 34
"Tragedy and the Common Man" by Arthur Miller from *The Viking Critical Library*. edited by Gerald Weales. Copyright 1949 by Arthur Miller. Reprinted by permission.

Supplemental Material
"Willy Loman Based on Real Uncle of Miller's" by Arthur Miller from *Timebends*, 1987. Reprinted with permission of the publisher, Grove Press, New York, New York.

Novel/Drama Series

Novel

Absolutely Normal Chaos/
 Chasing Redbird, Creech

Across Five Aprils, Hunt

Adam of the Road, Gray/Catherine,
 Called Birdy, Cushman

The Adventures of Huckleberry Finn,
 Twain

The Adventures of Tom Sawyer, Twain

Alice's Adventures in Wonderland/
 Through the Looking-Glass, Carroll

All Creatures Great and Small, Herriot

All Quiet on the Western Front,
 Remarque

All the King's Men, Warren

Animal Farm, Orwell/
 The Book of the Dun Cow,
 Wangerin, Jr.

Anna Karenina, Tolstoy

Anne Frank: The Diary of a Young Girl,
 Frank

Anne of Green Gables, Montgomery

April Morning, Fast

The Assistant/The Fixer, Malamud

The Autobiography of Miss Jane
 Pittman, Gaines

The Awakening, Chopin/
 Madame Bovary, Flaubert

Babbitt, Lewis

The Bean Trees/Pigs in Heaven,
 Kingsolver

Beowulf/Grendel, Gardner

Billy Budd/Moby Dick, Melville

Black Boy, Wright

Bless Me, Ultima, Anaya

Brave New World, Huxley

The Bridge of San Luis Rey, Wilder

The Brothers Karamazov, Dostoevsky

The Call of the Wild/White Fang,
 London

The Canterbury Tales, Chaucer

The Catcher in the Rye, Salinger

The Cay/Timothy of the Cay, Taylor

Charlotte's Web, White/
 The Secret Garden, Burnett

The Chosen, Potok

The Christmas Box, Evans/
 A Christmas Carol, Dickens

Chronicles of Narnia, Lewis

Cold Sassy Tree, Burns

The Count of Monte Cristo, Dumas

Crime and Punishment, Dostoevsky

Cry, the Beloved Country, Paton

Dandelion Wine, Bradbury

Darkness at Noon, Koestler

David Copperfield, Dickens

A Day No Pigs Would Die, Peck

Death Comes for the Archbishop,
 Cather

December Stillness, Hahn/
 Izzy, Willy-Nilly, Voigt

The Divine Comedy, Dante

The Dollmaker, Arnow

Don Quixote, Cervantes

Dr. Zhivago, Pasternak

Dubliners, Joyce

East of Eden, Steinbeck

Emma, Austen

Fahrenheit 451, Bradbury

A Farewell to Arms, Hemingway

Farewell to Manzanar, Houston &
 Houston/Black Like Me, Griffin

Frankenstein, Shelley

From the Mixed-up Files of Mrs. Basil
 E. Frankweiler, Konigsburg/The
 Westing Game, Raskin

A Gathering of Flowers, Thomas, ed.

The Giver, Lowry

The Good Earth, Buck

The Grapes of Wrath, Steinbeck

Great Expectations, Dickens

The Great Gatsby, Fitzgerald

Gulliver's Travels, Swift

Hard Times, Dickens

Hatchet, Paulsen/Robinson Crusoe,
 Defoe

The Heart Is a Lonely Hunter, McCullers

Heart of Darkness, Conrad

Hiroshima, Hersey/On the Beach, Shute

The Hobbit, Tolkien

Homecoming/Dicey's Song, Voigt

The Hound of the Baskervilles, Doyle

The Human Comedy/
 My Name Is Aram, Saroyan

Incident at Hawk's Hill, Eckert/
 Where the Red Fern Grows, Rawls

Invisible Man, Ellison

Jane Eyre, Brontë

Johnny Tremain, Forbes

Journey of the Sparrows, Buss &
 Cubias/The Honorable Prison, de
 Jenkins

The Joy Luck Club, Tan

Jubal Sackett/The Walking Drum,
 L'Amour

Julie of the Wolves, George/Island of
 the Blue Dolphins, O'Dell

The Jungle, Sinclair

The Killer Angels, Shaara

Le Morte D'Arthur, Malory

The Learning Tree, Parks

Les Miserables, Hugo

The Light in the Forest/
 A Country of Strangers, Richter

Little House in the Big Woods/
 Little House on the Prairie, Wilder

Little Women, Alcott

Lord of the Flies, Golding

The Lord of the Rings, Tolkien

The Martian Chronicles, Bradbury

Missing May, Rylant/The Summer of
 the Swans, Byars

Mrs. Mike, Freedman/I Heard the Owl
 Call My Name, Craven

Murder on the Orient Express/
 And Then There Were None, Christie

My Antonia, Cather

The Natural, Malamud/Shoeless Joe,
 Kinsella

Nectar in a Sieve, Markandaya/
 The Woman Warrior, Kingston

Night, Wiesel

A Night to Remember, Lord/Streams to
 the River, River to the Sea, O'Dell

1984, Orwell

Number the Stars, Lowry/Friedrich,
 Richter

Obasan, Kogawa

The Odyssey, Homer

The Old Man and the Sea,
 Hemingway/Ethan Frome, Wharton

The Once and Future King, White

O Pioneers!, Cather/The Country of
 the Pointed Firs, Jewett

Ordinary People, Guest/
 The Tin Can Tree, Tyler

The Outsiders, Hinton/
 Durango Street, Bonham

The Pearl/Of Mice and Men, Steinbeck

The Picture of Dorian Gray, Wilde/
 Dr. Jekyll and Mr. Hyde, Stevenson

The Pigman/The Pigman's Legacy,
 Zindel

A Portrait of the Artist as a Young Man, Joyce

The Power and the Glory, Greene

A Prayer for Owen Meany, Irving

Pride and Prejudice, Austen

The Prince, Machiavelli/Utopia, More

The Prince and the Pauper, Twain

Profiles in Courage, Kennedy

Rebecca, du Maurier

The Red Badge of Courage, Crane

The Return of the Native, Hardy

A River Runs Through It, Maclean

Roll of Thunder, Hear My Cry/
Let the Circle Be Unbroken, Taylor

Saint Maybe, Tyler

Sarum, Rutherfurd

The Scarlet Letter, Hawthorne

A Separate Peace, Knowles

Shabanu: Daughter of the Wind/
Haveli, Staples

Shane, Schaefer/The Ox-Bow
Incident, Van Tilburg Clark

Siddhartha, Hesse

The Sign of the Chrysanthemum/
The Master Puppeteer, Paterson

The Signet Classic Book of Southern
Short Stories, Abbott and
Koppelman, eds.

The Slave Dancer, Fox/
I, Juan de Pareja, De Treviño

Snow Falling on Cedars, Guterson

Song of Solomon, Morrison

The Sound and the Fury, Faulkner

Spoon River Anthology, Masters

A Stranger Is Watching/I'll Be Seeing
You, Higgins Clark

The Stranger/The Plague, Camus

Summer of My German Soldier, Greene/
Waiting for the Rain, Gordon

A Tale of Two Cities, Dickens

Talking God/A Thief of Time, Hillerman

Tess of the D'Urbervilles, Hardy

Their Eyes Were Watching God,
Hurston

Things Fall Apart/No Longer at Ease,
Achebe

To Kill a Mockingbird, Lee

To the Lighthouse, Woolf

Travels with Charley, Steinbeck

Treasure Island, Stevenson

A Tree Grows in Brooklyn, Smith

Tuck Everlasting, Babbitt/
Bridge to Terabithia, Paterson

The Turn of the Screw/Daisy Miller,
James

Uncle Tom's Cabin, Stowe

Walden, Thoreau/A Different
Drummer, Kelley

Walk Two Moons, Creech

Walkabout, Marshall

Watership Down, Adams

When the Legends Die, Borland

Where the Lilies Bloom, Cleaver/
No Promises in the Wind, Hunt

Winesburg, Ohio, Anderson

The Witch of Blackbird Pond, Speare/
My Brother Sam Is Dead, Collier
and Collier

A Wrinkle in Time, L'Engle/The Lion,
the Witch and the Wardrobe, Lewis

Wuthering Heights, Brontë

The Yearling, Rawlings/
The Red Pony, Steinbeck

Year of Impossible Goodbyes, Choi/So
Far from the Bamboo Grove, Watkins

Zlata's Diary, Filipović/
The Lottery Rose, Hunt

Drama

Antigone, Sophocles

Arms and the Man/Saint Joan, Shaw

The Crucible, Miller

Cyrano de Bergerac, Rostand

Death of a Salesman, Miller

A Doll's House/Hedda Gabler, Ibsen

The Glass Menagerie, Williams

The Importance of Being Earnest,
Wilde

Inherit the Wind, Lawrence and Lee

Long Day's Journey into Night, O'Neill

A Man for All Seasons, Bolt

Medea, Euripides/The Lion in Winter,
Goldman

The Miracle Worker, Gibson

Murder in the Cathedral, Eliot/Galileo,
Brecht

The Night Thoreau Spent in Jail,
Lawrence and Lee

Oedipus the King, Sophocles

Our Town, Wilder

The Playboy of the Western World/
Riders to the Sea, Synge

Pygmalion, Shaw

A Raisin in the Sun, Hansberry

1776, Stone and Edwards

She Stoops to Conquer, Goldsmith/
The Matchmaker, Wilder

A Streetcar Named Desire, Williams

Tartuffe, Molière

Three Comedies of American Family
Life: I Remember Mama, van
Druten/Life with Father, Lindsay
and Crouse/You Can't Take It with
You, Hart and Kaufman

Waiting for Godot, Beckett/
Rosencrantz & Guildenstern Are
Dead, Stoppard

Shakespeare

As You Like It

Hamlet

Henry IV, Part I

Henry V

Julius Caesar

King Lear

Macbeth

The Merchant of Venice

A Midsummer Night's Dream

Much Ado about Nothing

Othello

Richard III

Romeo and Juliet

The Taming of the Shrew

The Tempest

Twelfth Night

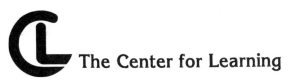
The Center for Learning

To Order Contact: **The Center for Learning—Shipping/Business Office**
P.O. Box 910, Villa Maria, PA 16155
800-767-9090 • 724-964-8083 • Fax 888-767-8080

The Publisher

All instructional materials identified by the TAP® (Teachers/ Authors/Publishers) trademark are developed by a national network of teachers whose collective educational experience distinguishes the publishing objective of The Center for Learning, a nonprofit educational corporation founded in 1970.

Concentrating on values-related disciplines, the Center publishes humanities and religion curriculum units for use in public and private schools and other educational settings. Approximately 500 language arts, social studies, novel/drama, life issues, and faith publications are available.

While acutely aware of the challenges and uncertain solutions to growing educational problems, the Center is committed to quality curriculum development and to the expansion of learning opportunities for all students. Publications are regularly evaluated and updated to meet the changing and diverse needs of teachers and students. Teachers may offer suggestions for development of new publications or revisions of existing titles by contacting

The Center for Learning

Administrative/Editorial Office
21590 Center Ridge Road
Rocky River, OH 44116
(440) 331-1404 • FAX (440) 331-5414
E-mail: cfl@stratos.net
Web: www.centerforlearning.org

For a free catalog containing order and price information and a descriptive listing of titles, contact

The Center for Learning

Shipping/Business Office
P.O. Box 910
Villa Maria, PA 16155
(724) 964-8083 • (800) 767-9090
FAX (888) 767-8080

Educator's Evaluation

The Center for Learning concept calls for frequent updates and revisions. Teachers writing for teachers will give us the best in instructional material.

Book Title_____

Excellent	Good	Fair	Poor	Criteria
				Overall effectiveness of the book
				Usability of the book
				Pacing of the material
				Quality of format and layout
				Availability of the selected text materials
				Student evaluation of the material
				Student motivation and interest
				Ability level of students
				Student achievement in the Unit

Used in Grade(s)_____

Used for
❏ Basic/Core for instruction
❏ Selected use
❏ Supplemental use

Teacher's experience
❏ 0-5 years
❏ 6-10 years
❏ 11-15 years
❏ 16 or more years

School Location
❏ large city
❏ suburb
❏ small town
❏ country

School Enrollment
❏ 1-499 students
❏ 500-999 students
❏ 1000 or more students

What is the greatest strength of this book?

What would you change in this book?

Additional Comments:

Name_____

Position_____

School_____

Address_____

Please return to:

The Center for Learning
21590 Center Ridge Rd.
Rocky River, Ohio 44116